**Forewords by
BOB PROCTOR & JACK M. ZUFELT**

SUCCEED with IMPOSSIBLE SPEED

World Class Racing Strategies to Create High Performance in Your Life and Business

EDRICK DUNAND

All Rights Reserved

© 2010 by Edrick Dunand

This book may not be reproduced in whole or in part, by any means, without written consent of the publisher.

LIFESUCCESS PUBLISHING, LLC

8900 E Pinnacle Peak Road, Suite D240
Scottsdale, AZ, 85255

Telephone: 800.473.7134
Fax: 480.661.1014
E-mail: admin@lifesuccesspublishing.com

ISBN: 978-1-59930-344-4

Cover: Lloyd Arbour, LifeSuccess Publishing, LLC
Text: Lloyd Arbour, LifeSuccess Publishing, LLC

Photo Credit: Dan R. Boyd

Edit: Publication Services

COMPANIES, ORGANIZATIONS, INSTITUTIONS, AND INDUSTRY PUBLICATIONS. Quantity discounts are available on bulk purchases of this book for reselling, educational purposes, subscription incentives, gifts, sponsorship, or fundraising. Special books or book excerpts can also be created to fit specific needs such as private labeling with your logo on the cover and a message from a VIP printed inside. For more information, please contact our Special Sales Department at LifeSuccess Publishing, LLC.

DEDICATION

To the most precious people on planet earth - my family:

Jo Anne, Joshua, Tessa and Sommer.

To those who are hungry and thirsty to live life more abundantly, and are not afraid to expand their borders.

Above all, to the one who is directing my steps: my Father in Heaven who through his son Jesus-Christ brought me to Himself and gave me the desire to seek out daily the ways of wisdom and grow in high performance living.

ACKNOWLEDGEMENTS

Success is a team affair. I extend my most grateful appreciation and admiration to my beautiful bride and true partner for life: my wife Jo Anne. You have given me the greatest gift a man can receive: your trust in me and faith in my destiny. Your patience and presence in the birthing of this book, your love and support makes you the invisible but ever present co-writer of this book – It would have been only impossible without you.

A unique thank you to my son Joshua for being such a powerful inspiration. Your maturity, your personal and racing talents are very special, and your creative mindset will cause you to be a leader in your generation. As we grow together into the realisation of our common vision and purpose, no matter what lays in the future, on and off the racing track, I will be forever very proud of you.

My dear daughter Tessa has been a unique contributor through her creation of "impossible speed" crafts which populate my office. Your very fine spirit and acute mind make you a superb listener and challenger of ideas. Your destiny can only be extraordinary as you truly are a gift to the world.

Sommer you were wonderful in letting Daddy hide in his office for so many hours. Your unconditional support and spontaneous cheering along the way made a world of difference. Your shiny character and beautiful heart will never cease to amaze me. You are so uniquely gifted that you cannot but touch the world just by being there.

To the whole team at Life Success Publishing; Dee Burks who made available her expertise and suffered reading through my early writings, Lloyd Arbour and his strong artistic talents, George Parachou for his energy and commitment to deliver success.

My most affectionate thanks go to my dearest friends: John Sessions for being such a confident believer and powerful supporter throughout the entire acceleration process of Impossible Speed and to this day, and to Jill Klein whose prayers, support and insight form an often invisible but powerful shield of strength. My heartfelt gratitude to my faithful friend Alan Woodhouse, whose friendship, wisdom and knowledge have profoundly impacted my life and given so much to build upon.

Resounding thanks to all my friends in the racing world who have allowed me to enter and develop in this wonderful world of High Performance and learn so much in a short period of time.

CONTENTS

FOREWORDS		13
PREFACE		17
INTRODUCTION		21
PART 1:	YOU WERE BORN A CHAMPION	25
Chapter 1	Leaving the Bleachers	26
Chapter 2	Test Drive	29
Chapter 3	Racing Your Own Race	32
Chapter 4	Sitting in the Cockpit	35
Chapter 5	Switch on the Ignition	38
PART 2:	FROM SEDAN TO PROTOTYPE	41
Chapter 6	Le Mans Prototype Design	42
Chapter 7	Race Engine	46
Chapter 8	Change of Gears	49
Chapter 9	Facets of Speed	53
Chapter 10	Racing Allies	56
Chapter 11	Comfort to Performance	60
PART 3:	RACING LINES	63
Chapter 12	Driving and Racing	64
Chapter 13	Decision and Reflection	69
Chapter 14	Commitment to High Performance	74

■ RACING STRATEGIES TO CREATE HIGH PERFORMANCE

Chapter 15	Points of No Return	77
Chapter 16	Boldness versus Hesitancy	79
Chapter 17	High-Speed Blind Turns	81
Chapter 18	Dry and Wet Lines	84

PART 4:	RACING STRATEGY	87
Chapter 19	Going for Gold	88
Chapter 20	Racing Plan	91
Chapter 21	Control	99
Chapter 22	Racing to the Finish Line	101
Chapter 23	Rookie Racing	103
Chapter 24	Racing Mentors	105

PART 5:	THE RACER'S EDGE	109
Chapter 25	Special Breed	110
Chapter 26	The Complete Driver	112
Chapter 27	The Championship Mindset	117
Chapter 28	Race Conditioning	119
Chapter 29	Hand-Eye Coordination	122
Chapter 30	Befriending Risk	123

PART 6:	WHEN THINGS GO WRONG	129
Chapter 31	Crash	130
Chapter 32	Racing after the Crash	134
Chapter 33	Caught in Traffic	137
Chapter 34	Not Quite Yet	143

PART 7:	RACE FUEL	147
Chapter 35	Your Most Important Investment	148
Chapter 36	Racing Budget	153
Chapter 37	Partnerships	155
Chapter 38	Octane or Oxygen	161

PART 8:	RACING TO WIN!	165
Chapter 39	Qualifying	166
Chapter 40	Great Start	169
Chapter 41	Adjusting Your Race Pace	173
Chapter 42	Clean Racing	176
Chapter 43	Press in and Take It Away	181

PART 9:	RACE TEAM POWER	185
Chapter 44	Your Team, Your Win	187
Chapter 45	Team Leadership	191
Chapter 46	Team Communications	194
Chapter 47	Everyone Counts	197

PART 10:	SETTING UP FOR RACE DAY	201
Chapter 48	Data Analysis	202
Chapter 49	Oversteering, Understeering	207
Chapter 50	The Circle of Grip	210
Chapter 51	Speed or Down Force	214
Chapter 52	Watching the Clock	217

BONUS: **221**
INTERVIEW WITH TERRY BORCHELLER
Winner of the 2010 ROLEX 24 at Daytona

FOREWORD *BOB PROCTOR*

One of the most exciting endeavors we can embark on is to expand who and what we can be. Even the most erudite scientist alive would be hard pressed to quantify our potential – it's infinite.

There's a wonderful quote by Steve Bow, "God's gift to you is more talent and ability than you will ever use in one lifetime. Your gift to God is to develop and utilize as much of that talent and ability as you can, in this lifetime." Edrick Dunand has done a remarkable job using his racing experience to help people understand how to super charge their lives and develop their potential.

Each one of us has the power to choose how we view the world and how we react to the circumstances in our lives. Just like navigating the twists and turns on a race track, we can choose to prepare ourselves to succeed or allow life to happen to us. Edrick writes, "Imagine being one with your vision for your life, totally strapped in, nowhere else to go, nowhere else you would rather be. Your high-performance life can take you there really fast with tremendous acceleration, because it is not just any car, it is a vehicle made to race, just like you were born to live to the fullest."

For more than four decades I've dedicated my life to the study of human potential. There are many parallels between training for success in life and training for success on the racetrack – both deal with the mind. *Succeed with Impossible Speed* is a wonderful example of how you can use the power of your mind to build the life you dream of and to overcome those obstacles that stand in your way. By understanding what motivates us as individuals, we can gain an awareness of how to reach our next level of performance but this doesn't happen automatically.

Edrick Dunand reveals the steps and strategies that will take your life to new heights and allow you to achieve more than you ever dreamed possible. *Succeed with Impossible Speed* is the catalyst to help you move from mediocre results to a new world of prosperity and happiness.

This book will be the starting point of a new awareness and confidence that will bring you the emotional, physical and spiritual richness that you desire.

—Bob Proctor
Best Selling author of *You Were Born Rich*
Chairman, LifeSuccess Group of Companies

FOREWORD *JACK M. ZUFELT*

I like this book!

Edrick Dunand has written a book that can make you a winner in life…and *fast*! There are two ways to make things happen…slow and fast. Everyone wants things to happen fast. This book will show you how to do that.

If you have the desire to accelerate your success rate, in any area of life, read "Succeed with Impossible Speed" and you will learn how to go from slow to fast in all that you do.

Edrick uses his vast experience in the racing world to bring very interesting, powerful examples, analogies and stories from the exciting and popular world of professional racing into your life in a way that will show you how to experience *high speed* success.

Many people enter the race of marriage, business or life in general but don't even cross the finish line let alone be a winner. If you want to dramatically accelerate your ability to make things happen and cross the finish line as a high speed winner then read this book as fast as you can.

If you are stuck or feel like you have a flat tire, your engine is not firing on all cylinders, this book can change all that so you can become a peak performer and quickly.

As an internationally recognized success expert, I can say that Edrick has done a great job of explaining how to get out of neutral or low gear and shift into high gear so you can make success happen faster than you ever dreamed possible.

When you do this you will be able to achieve all your Core Desires!

READ IT NOW!

—Jack M. Zufelt
"Mentor To Millions"
Author of the #1 bestselling book, *The DNA of Success*,
International Keynote Speaker and Trainer
www.dnaofsuccess.com
www.jackzufeltspeaks.com

PREFACE

Whether you are looking for personal answers, leadership solutions, or career related questions, this book was written for you. It exposes some powerful success principles to cause you to succeed in a brand-new way – the Impossible Speed way.

There is a general perception that we tend to live somewhat below our real abilities regardless of our level of success and achievement. There are only a few people who demonstrate high levels of "complete achievement" personally and professionally. It is important to notice that these successful people have a different perspective on achievement than less successful individuals. They never seem to have reached their limits and are in a constant motion of growth: they live in a creative dynamic of life, and they adapt and redirect constantly in a dance of persistence and determination. Just like a race driver leads the race car from corner to corner, forever adjusting to the ever-changing conditions of the race track, they, too, are always on the lookout for maximum performance.

There is a clear purpose in these pages: to give you effective knowledge and understanding towards accelerating the results in your life, in your business, and in all that truly matters to you. As such, this book is dedicated to the men and women who have an open mind and are hungry for greater levels of achievement, not only at work or in their business or careers, but also in their overall quality of life.

Succeed with Impossible Speed is not meant to be solely a catchy title; it is the experience of many people, including me. You, too, will see that you can create so much change in your life in such a short period of time that it can truly amaze you.

Together we will go on a journey that is meant to impact your life positively and contribute to giving you more of the things that you really want and much less of those that you really do not want at all.

I have personally read and studied dozens of books as well as listened to dozens of courses and attended many seminars on personal and leadership development. I have gleaned many gems of wisdom from great mentors who have already walked the walk of growth and success.

However, there has been a recurring phenomenon: my transport to new levels of hope to bring change and more results to my life seemed to be doomed to return to base even though I wanted to climb. I experienced slowdowns and setbacks that seemed to oppose my acceleration towards achieving my goals and objectives. All of this was an object of disappointment and frustration until I learned the concepts and ideas that I am sharing with you in this book.

In order to give a clear perception of the principles explored and empower you to retain them and make them your own for life, we are going to learn something quite extraordinary. The very principles that govern the exercise of the sport of high-performance car racing are the same universal principles that will cause you to succeed at an extraordinary level.

High-performance racing typifies the success principles that we are about to look into. Knowingly or unknowingly, many drivers and teams have harnessed these principles to produce the most fantastic racing exploits. You will find this book to be much more than a metaphorical parallel, as it will give you the means to identify high-performance formulas to create the transformation you need. In fact, I am quite confident that although you may not be a racing enthusiast, you will be amazed to discover the world of hidden treasures of understanding that emanates from the spectacular sport of race-car driving and all that it encompasses.

Although I love many forms of motor racing, we will be focusing on the extraordinary resources of world-class racing and primarily the American Le Mans Series. Why?

Any venture is to be led by example, and Dr. Don Panoz, chairman of the Panoz Automotive Group, is a model of outstanding vision and leadership. Dr. Panoz conducted a visionary charge in 1999 to bring to America a new racing series imported from Europe and inspired by the legendary 24 hours of Le Mans. It required boldness that few can display and sustain. Scott Atherton, CEO of the ALMS, displayed remarkable leadership, allowing Dr. Panoz's vision to become reality. Today, the American Le Mans is synonymous with world-class achievements with many prestigious world-class racing teams, including many car manufacturers such as Audi, Aston Martin, BMW, Dodge, General Motors, Ferrari, Ford, Mazda, Panoz, and Porsche.

There are also three specific characteristics that make ALMS the ideal background of leadership development. First, American Le Mans, like life, is not a sprint race but more an endurance race. Second, the level of human performance to achieve what is needed throughout the race series is nothing short of breathtaking and highly inspiring. Third, the openness of the series to be relevant to the world of its fans makes it the ideal partner to help you map out your own extraordinary success journey.

ARE YOU READY TO "SUCCEED WITH IMPOSSIBLE SPEED"?

LET'S GO FOR IT!

INTRODUCTION

Often I am asked: "Where are you from?" Although I am an ordinary Canadian citizen in our multicultural country, what obviously intrigues people is to find out, after my accent gives me away, where I was born. Whether we like it or not, our origins strongly influence the makeup of our lives.

I was born in France, in a beautiful historical city called Lyon. Lyon is the French capital of gastronomy and is surrounded by several vineyard regions. Once people find out that I was born in France, they always ask: "Why did you move? Do you like it here?" Are you kidding? I don't like it; I love it! And the number-one reason that I love it is because Canada is the birth country of my beautiful wife, Jo Anne. She had the courage as a young adult to follow her dreams and to come live in France, where we had the opportunity to meet. At the time, she was working in our little evangelical church; then she became my wife and the mother of our three extraordinary children.

Another reason that leads me to love Canada and North America at large is that I feel at home like I never felt anywhere in Europe. My belief is that although where we come from is important and cannot ever be concealed, where we are and, moreover, where we are going is even more important.

I grew up in a multigenerational family business in which I was expected from my earliest days to become the successor. This assumption about my future was to prove costly as I found myself awakening in my twenties to the painful reality of having no sense of identity of my own, other than my family's reputation and image. I did my best to fit in, trying to wear the mantle of succession. I even initiated a new company of my own to try to give it my personal touch, but I failed miserably. I could not deliver any substantial results, as I was trying to fill a role in which I found myself having the vague mirror image of my parents but no authenticity towards myself.

I don't know if this sounds remotely familiar to you, but I meet so many people who, over time, have little sense of personal definition and are left with a "heart" or "life" ache that does not seem to go away.

My happiest years as a teenager were spent competing in Motocross and Enduro racing. I was not content enough to ride; I needed to compete and measure myself against the competition. I trained with some of the best European competitors and was quite successful on a regional level until a training accident put an end to my quest. After six years of competitive riding, I had tasted high performance, and I chose car-rally racing to feed my growing passion for motor racing.

I enrolled in a rally school in Nevers, in rural central France, region of Bourgogne, and it was a complete revelation. What I had learned about everyday driving had nothing to do with race driving, and I was discovering the hidden world of high-speed control. I raced a few hill climbs and rallies and accumulated a few podium finishes. I was full of hope for my bright racing future until I crashed my car at a fairly high speed, which resulted in massive damage. As a one-man operation, this was a big deal. Although I reengineered and upgraded the performance of my Volkswagen Golf GTI Group N to a Group A, I never really got back to rally racing. It was a time of personal and spiritual discovery that led me to question the validity of my purpose in wanting to race. As I started doubting, my confidence started eroding. I could no longer dare to believe that I could be a good racer. The final blow came as I missed being selected in a factory junior-selection program. It was enough to cause me to totally stop believing. My racing dreams had come to a grinding halt, and I had simply given up.

Fast forward ten years. In 1996, I arrived in Canada with my wife and my firstborn son, Joshua. From there, nothing would be the same again, as I was given an extraordinary chance at choosing a new life in a new country. I could now reset all of the dials of my life, one by one. I had just completed my initial training stages as a commercial pilot, and I used that to engage passionately in a successful career in aviation sales and aviation management. Five years later I found myself struggling, as the aircraft-market economy was very challenged in the new millennium. In spite of my love for airplanes, I was ready to take on a new challenge: to reconcile work and family life.

Once again I was successful and quickly joined the ranks of top sales performers at one of the largest and oldest Education Savings Plan providers in the country. Ranking in the top 2 per cent of the sales force in a short two-year period after joining the company was a commendable achievement. I was delighted to have finally achieved my desired goal to control my schedule, have a good business income, and put my family first. What I did not know is that I was about to embark on a life-altering journey.

PART 1
YOU WERE BORN A CHAMPION

LEAVING THE BLEACHERS

CHAPTER 1

That particular Sunday of June 2005 was solely dedicated to entertaining my three young children. My wife was away for the weekend on a speaking engagement with a group of ladies from our church. We decided to enjoy a brunch with Joshua, our firstborn, who was only nine years old at the time. Tessa and Sommer, my two little princesses, were just barely six and five, respectively. Afterwards we drove to what I believed was a Kart racing event at the renowned track of Shannonville in Ontario, Canada. Joshua had been asking to buy a motocross, but I was concerned based on my personal experience. I wanted to introduce him to a form of motorsports that he would enjoy and that would not expose him to undue risk of injury. Alas, there was no Kart racing but rather was car racing of some regional series.

We roamed nonchalantly through the paddock, looking at various types of race machines. Joshua was even invited to sit in the compact cockpit of a Formula 2000 by its young driver. Joshua looked quite small, but believe me the grin on his face was not! After that entertaining episode, we walked towards the bleachers that overlook the track running across the Canadian countryside. The temperature was quite hot, yet to my surprise my two little girls seemed quite content and even found it funny to watch these strange and noisy things going by so fast.

My own mind started to get into gear, and I became irresistibly involved with the race. The race-driving lessons that I had taken nearly 20 years earlier seemed to come back to life, and before long I wondered how I would be doing in that race. I could feel an internal voice saying to me, "You would be very good at this." I promptly dismissed it. I had matured into a responsible husband and father and had no intention of going backwards. Anyway, there was no point in struggling with it as I did not have any funds available for it – end of story!

As we prepared to leave the track, a pleasant gentleman offered the children some posters. He was a racer, and he introduced himself as John Bondard, president of a regional racing series called Canadian Automobile Sports Club of Ontario. He was doing a good promotional job of enticing me to join the series – did he read my mind? I found myself playing the game, giving echo to my persisting inner voice that kept saying, "You would be good at this."

As the conversation progressed, I came to realise that, despite what I thought, I had not forgotten anything of my racing past; it had simply been deactivated for a long while. My connection to racing had been put to sleep but had never ceased to be.

Driving home, I felt unexplainable joy and excitement. Although I was not even planning to race again, something special started to beat inside of me with trepidation. I certainly did not give it this meaning at the time, but later I would realize that I had crossed paths with destiny.

In the days that followed, my racing thoughts kept strengthening. I did not have the smallest idea how I would ever race again; my finances did not quite allow me to do so. There was one feeling, however, growing stronger and faster than others; I was not born to watch but to live and experience life to the fullest. I was born to be part of the race. I was born a racer! I was born a champion, regardless of my racing future. My desire to live the life that I was born to live had irreversibly taken over.

In the weeks and months that followed, a new process took a life of its own. What if racing was not limited to fun and excitement; what if it was really part of my life, part of my makeup, part of my identity? Identity? It was a mystery that I had tried to solve for myself for too long, probably since I was in my early teens.

Where is that special place for me, what am I here for, is there anything special about me? What do I really want? Do I even have any desire powerful enough to move me though obstacles and lead me to a place of achievement that will be totally satisfactory, a life that will be meaningful, and a purpose that will be significant?

I had been on life's bleachers for too long, and I did not want to watch anymore; I wanted to be in the action, to live it, experience it. I wanted to feel deep inside of me that I was at the right place, at the right time, doing the right thing, and be very good at it. Everything in me was now calling out and telling me that I was born to live my very own success story. Even better, this race of life was not meant to be for me alone but to positively affect my relationship with my whole family, and particularly, to build the ultimate dream team: a father and a son racing with a common objective and a common purpose.

Before I had even begun my journey, it had become clear to me that engaging into my life success story was meant to extend way beyond myself and my family. My racing story would, in its time, inspire others to leave their own life bleachers and get engaged in their own life success race.

Now equipped with the real picture in mind, the race was ready to begin - on and off the race track.

TEST DRIVE

CHAPTER 2

When the student is ready, the teacher appears. Such a man came into my life a few years ago: Alan Woodhouse. He is a personal coach extraordinaire and has become a dear friend of mine. He taught me to accept that there was tremendous value in all that had made up my life to this very day. Yes, even those things that I viewed as total failures. This was no simplistic positive thinking but rather an opportunity to understand that there was a thread running through life that had been formed through all the ups and downs. If I was willing, I could follow it, and it could help me find the life that I was looking for.

Let's face it: regrets are of a very unproductive nature. Looking back at the making of our lives, we should not let regret invade our present. Now, I know that for some people who have experienced traumatic events, this may be rather difficult, and I am sensitive to that. However, for myself, I had to accept unconditionally that my past was gone forever. Therefore, there was no point worrying about it. It was now my choice to either hold on to hurtful thoughts and feelings or to start salvaging what I could use and throw out the rest. However difficult it might be, we cannot move forward while entertaining regrets that are usually expressed in the form of "if" and "if only".

As I was writing these pages, a racing story caught my attention: his name is Mikko Hirvonen. He is not an American Le Mans racer but rather the 2009 vice–world champion in the WRC (world rally championship) to now six-times consecutive world champion, Frenchman Sebastien

Loeb. Loeb and his Citroën Factory team finished the championship with a single-point lead. Yes, Mikko is not world champion because of a single missing point. Imagine this, thousands of hours of work, hundreds of hours driving at a lightning speed on timed special, overcoming countless obstacles, and escaping innumerable dangerous situations to finish one point short, missing out on the prize. In a recent interview, Mikko Hirvonen said: "It's more frustrating that I didn't make a single mistake and he [Loeb] made three and still managed to pull it away."

There must be plenty of regret material in Mikko Hirvonen's thoughts, speaking in the form of "what if" and "if only". These thoughts would involve him, of course, but also his factory Ford Rally racing team as he replays in the theatre of his mind the various races of the year that took place all over the globe. Yes, so many possible regrets in hindsight.

However, as a true champion, Hirvonen is not lingering in the past. On the contrary, he looks at the year ahead, not with the dread of repeating the past but with great anticipation of taking ownership of his shortfall and mishap as well as success and victories. With a determined attitude to do better next time, Mikko says, "I need to be braver."

The opposite end of the spectrum of regrets is gratitude. Gratitude can overcome many of the worst emotions – even the worst regrets. I became grateful as I learned that everything in my life, including struggles, shortfalls, and attempts and failures, had participated in forming my skills and strengths of today. To create impossible speed, you need great power, and a lot of it would come into my life and business in direct connection with my personal response to my circumstances. It is no longer about the circumstances themselves, as I now have the opportunity to look at my life with the perspective of finding the power angle and to extract value for my own life.

In my teenage years and as a student, I never really wanted to learn mechanical engineering, as I never thought it would be useful or lead me anywhere I wanted to go. However, since I did not know what I wanted, other than the family prescription of succession to the family business, I ended up trying it anyway. Today I have learned to appreciate and be grateful that the systematic approach to mechanisms that I developed in these studies has been an asset to many aspects of my business endeavours.

Although my first business start-up was not the expected success that I wanted it to be, it built in me many of the drivers powering up my various enterprises today. I did not manage to become a professional pilot like I once dreamed of, but my private flying experience, combined with my knowledge of business, opened doors that would have otherwise been closed when I moved to Canada and had to start my life all over again. I could comment on every struggle and every diversion that I've had to date, all of which contain a part of my current positive and effective life puzzle. These experiences created my life, and I have become grateful for them.

I used to resent and complain a lot. I did for a long time, and still can experience occasional relapse! Why did my parents not understand me better, why could I not come up with my own sense of personal direction earlier, why did I not manage this development step or succeed at that point in time? Actually, for many years, I thought there was something really wrong with me. I had to understand that my personal beliefs and my paradigms were in need of adjustment. Blaming my past and others was an obvious liability and a heavy weight to carry around. So I chose to let go of that liability and travel lighter.

Imagine if someone had told me when I was in high school trying to learn German as a second language, with no clue about my direction in life: "You will one day author a book on self-development and life-acceleration strategies that will help people live lives of purpose and greater effectiveness. And that book will be written in English; you will write it as a Canadian citizen while you progress in your racing career." Trust me; I would have called the people in white coats to dispose of the deluded person promptly.

RACING YOUR OWN RACE

CHAPTER 3

Acquiring a sense of identity, purpose, and direction for our lives should not be complicated if we train in the way we should go from childhood. However, if you are like me, it probably did not happen. So now we have to give definition to our lives ourselves. On the journey to a high-performance life, we start with a backpack full of personal history, loaded with all kinds of beliefs, saturated with emotions, and dominated by awkward feelings as we often snack on very unproductive thoughts of failure and regrets. We become captive of our quest instead of becoming forthcoming and victorious in generating our desired results.

Do you know that it is easy to hide in complexities instead of coming out in the open to find real solutions?

A simple procedure changed my view on this and allowed me to quite easily find out the "big picture" of who Edrick is. I even discovered some very specific pointers that do not leave much room for guesswork. What a pleasure it is to switch the lights on! However, before jumping into the "how to", it is important to acquire the right mindset about this. As it goes with any prize, there is a cost attached to acquiring a clear sense of definition of your identity and purpose. Becoming aware of your unique life identity and your success DNA is going to form a solution that will potentially trigger some serious inner conflicts. You will experience unprecedented joy in your life, but you are also going to be challenged to act upon your newfound knowledge; no more hiding in the dark. Only in action is our faith and courage really put to the test. Once you find your life's blueprint, once it is in front of you, once you perceive and even touch and feel it, you must stop fighting against it, take immediate action, and start putting it into form.

In this self-discovery approach, I discovered that my love for piloting fast machines (motorcycles-cars-airplanes) was not a fantasy but a thread of my personal identity. This was no teenage impulse or fad; it was a genuine part of my heart's desire. When something is in place as a piece of your life identity puzzle or success DNA, you cannot nor should you attempt to turn away from it. Rather, you should embrace it enthusiastically and love it unconditionally in order to start living it to its fullest potential as you progress one step at a time.

Another element that I discovered is that it was important for me to have a sense of rightness and purpose in all that I do. Doing things for the fun of it is not enough; I want the full depth of anything I venture into, not just the quick reward. I found that contributing to other people out of my own success was a major piece of my personal identity. As you may imagine, this discovery naturally led to the writing of this book, and the forming of the Amaris Group – our leadership development company.

We all have genius as part of our unique makeup. It is virtually impossible to not be aware of others' genius, but it is easy to denigrate our own and fall short of the life we truly want, simply accepting our lot in resignation. We must acknowledge our special talents, the things we are good at, the activities and subjects that unleash passion in our hearts. It is a must because they are a gift to us to define our very DNA of our own success and fulfilment. No one would ever trample a beautiful garden or throw away treasures of gold and other precious metal. Yet, day in and day out, we ransack our own hearts and minds with our damaging thoughts that tell us we are incapable of rising above our present level of living for all kinds of so-called logical reasons.

You must acknowledge today, that there is only one "you" and that regardless of how you feel about yourself right now, you are an authentic, unique, and glorious reality! One day "*you*" was born, and before "*you*" was born, "*you*" had to be created, because "*you*" did not exist yet prior to that time of creation. "*You*" is a unique piece of the created world, a unique piece of craftsmanship, and a unique reality. By investing more time in your wonderful reality, you will learn to give a new dynamic dimension to your life. Soon, armed with the specific knowledge of your talents and abilities, undeterred from living to the full the meaningful desires of your heart, and responding to the echo of your very own DNA for high performance, "*you*" will start experiencing a life of a truly surprising nature.

Your life is your race; only you can race it. Only you can drive it, and only you can bring influence at the wheel. You alone can make the decision to leave the bleachers, take your place on the track, and start racing towards genuine fulfilment.

Interestingly, the more you make room for yourself, the more you will understand your need for healthy and harmonious relationships with others. High-performance racing is a team endeavour, not lone-ranger bliss. Although only the driver is at the wheel to execute the race, there is a whole team with equal responsibility for his victory. You will race for yourself and your team, but never by yourself or all about yourself.

Take heart; there is a whole crew out there to help you make it happen!

SITTING IN THE COCKPIT

CHAPTER 4

When I sit in the cockpit of a race car or even in one of our sprint race karts, I am immediately transported into another world, a world that I treasure dearly. The first thing that you notice when you sit in a race car is that everything is purposely designed for performance, not for relaxation and comfort. Everything must have a particular function for competing at the highest level, and anything unnecessary to the performance goal must go.

Come with me and imagine snuggling in the tight cockpit of a Formula car or of a Le Mans prototype. You don't just sit in it like you do in your road car. You have to snuggle into your race car, fit in it, and become a part of the machine to be able to deliver high-speed racing. You slide inside by wiggling your way in, as you are surrounded by the rugged functionality of the cockpit. Once you are seated, you strap yourself firmly in place with a five-point harness made of large belts pressing over your body. This is not only to aid in case of accident, it is a necessity in order for the driver to stay "one" with the race vehicle as you drive at a high pace – otherwise your body would be thrown around with resulting loss of control. You can do nothing but reach your steering wheel, your pedals, and needed switches and controls – you don't want more mobility anymore; you now welcome this restraint, which is reassuring. You have now become physically one with your race vehicle.

Imagine being one with your vision for your life, totally strapped in, nowhere else to go, nowhere else you would rather be. You can't wiggle anymore; you can't get out without voluntarily unfastening the tight snug of the belts. At that point, you go where the car goes and vice versa. Your high-performance life can take you there really fast with tremendous acceleration, because it is not just any car, it is a vehicle made to race, just like you were born to live to the fullest.

As you sit on the grid, even before the ignition is switched on, your eyes do only one natural thing: look ahead, where the track is unfolding in front of you. Your hands are on the steering wheel awaiting your input as you focus ahead with intensity. Your race vehicle will respond with superior accuracy to any move that you choose to make.

Imagine if you could direct your life with the same accuracy as a race vehicle, with its direct and responsive steering. That is where vision comes in, as you steer only where you know you really want to go. This is why knowing what you want is so important. Your life's vision is like the open race track ahead. Your own clarity will dictate your visibility level, and you will need it. Why? Trust me, once your race vehicle is unleashed, once it is accelerating, gaining speed and momentum, pinning you in the race seat, your life is going to unfold at vertiginous speed towards the realisation of your goals.

The average person cannot run much faster than 20-25 km/hr for a few seconds, but when strapped into a race vehicle, we become able to reach heart-stopping speed creating a sense of freedom and power. Likewise, when you strap yourself in with your life's vision, you will not only start moving forward but you will reach previously unthinkable speeds of achievement.

On the other side of the coin, if you try to take a race car into commuter traffic to work, it will rattle, shake and overheat while making you the driver totally miserable. You will likewise be out of place and shaken by the vibrations of a frustrated life, if you fail to identify your life direction. Just like the race vehicle is made to do one thing- accelerate and go fast, you must create your own open track to accelerate towards the results you really want.

When you think acceleration, your worst enemy in going out in the open is called the "comfort zone". This may feel safe: not taking much risk, not going too far from familiar territories, not venturing into anything too different or challenging. Just keep doing what you have always done and leave it at that, including the frustrations that go with it. This is not the life you are meant to live; it falls short of your potential, short of dreams and aspirations, short of joy, happiness, and fulfilment, and short of achievements. The comfort zone is more like a death zone in disguise. It is so much a part of your life that you cannot imagine how to get away from it. You must get out at all cost. How? Listen to your heart, and trust that your desires were given not to create regrets and nostalgia but to cause you to spring forth, breaking down the doors of the jail of the comfort zone. You can never race in confined spaces or traffic jams.

You need to find your way out of too much traffic and not enough performance. You have to decide to let yourself take a fresh turn, a total life makeover if necessary. This said, you need to learn to drive before you can race. You need to learn this new life process before you can accelerate. And it starts with the master key: the decision to switch on the ignition.

You can be strapped into the most powerful race vehicle, ready to go, with all the technology and all the power available to you, for your command, for your input – but until you are ready to flip that switch, nothing will happen.

Life is waiting for your most powerful command: "Yes, let's do it, switch it on!"

SWITCH ON THE IGNITION

CHAPTER 5

There is something outright magical about switches. When you switch something on, it immediately transitions from one state to another. When you flip on a light switch in your house, a room that once was dark is now full of light. When you switch on your race vehicle, the dormant power plant now comes to life and is ready to burst forward. This sound of power brought to life in a race engine creates an indescribable feeling in a split second! When you make a supportive life decision for yourself in alignment with your "true heart's desire", something suddenly comes alive within you. The change is so sudden that it might be unsettling. The life power plant that was dormant within you is now coming to life.

For me, there have been many switching-on events in my life. You will find many switches on the dashboard of your race car, and they are all important, but there is only one master switch. The master switch controls and authorises the release of the power. When you switch on your race vehicle, you are going to authorise many processes to come to life. It is all about decision! Decision is a golden word in the dictionary of high performance and success. In real estate, it is first about location, second about location, third about location. In high-performance living, it is about decision, decision, decision. Good and proper decisions cause all of the functions of your life to come together and give you the motion forward that you need. Decisions are the fruit of three things: acknowledgement of desire, willingness to move in the direction of the realisation of that desire, and commitment to stay the course until the desired result is obtained.

Sometimes I can find myself in a tight race and under pressure from my opponents. The fatigue starts to settle in, my focus diminishes, and the pleasure of the moment tends to fade and be replaced by the pain of enduring until the finish line. It is obvious that this is no time to switch off. And yet, what do we do in our lives when things get tough? We tend to switch off. You may tell yourself, "I told you it was not going to work"; "There was no way I could save this marriage"; "There is no way I could pursue my vision and my dreams; it is just too hard"; and you switch off. There are many times, even in the process of publishing this book while all other demands press on me, that I myself am tempted to consider the cost more than the end result – the finish line. Is it worth it? Is it going to work? Where am I going to get the significant financial resources needed to finance the progression of our racing team with my son? What if it stalls, what if my dream comes to a halt? What if I was wrong?

Have you ever had that paralysing experience of when doubts set in and you are tempted to yield to the pressure of failure even before you start building a solution? It may in your finances, in your relationship at home or at work. It may be that weight loss you want so badly seems so far out, or you dread failing in a new business that you want to start. You ask yourself – should I go for it or not?

We all have had this experience in one way or another. But in all of the types of decisions that we make, there is only one kind of decision that will survive the test of time and fatigue; it is a decision that comes from the knowledge of your heart's desire, which you know is good and true and will serve a noble purpose. It is a decision that is irrevocable and unchangeable, and it will cause you to give it all that you have. When decisions contain that much intensity and resolution, you will become unable to stop no matter how great the temporary pain may be. All successful people have been able to endure before they can enjoy. Opposition, however, is never meant to push you out, but to qualify you for the prize.

Unfortunately, too many people make weak decisions because their focus is too conditional. Their primary concern is protection from failure, staying in or close to the comfort zone. In such a condition, the decisions made are not real decisions; they are just trials and attempts, a mere shadow of real decisions. A real decision causes you to move forward even though it may be hard. Making that business work, saving a marriage, helping a child change in order to overcome his or her difficulties, getting out of financial strain – none of them have short fixes or answers. There is only one worthwhile way to go about it, one form of decision to be taken: decide to win. A real decision is called a total commitment. It is a solemn promise to yourself that you will do whatever it takes until it has fully materialised.

Only this kind of decision, with its burning intensity, will give you the power to succeed and achieve your highest desires with impossible speed.

PART 2
FROM SEDAN TO PROTOTYPE

LE MANS PROTOTYPE DESIGN

CHAPTER 6

The way you were created is totally extraordinary. Throughout the ages, philosophers and religious people have disagreed about many things, yet everyone points to a direct connection between the inner condition of people and their experience of life. From Aristotle to Einstein, from biblical scriptures to modern research on cognitive behaviour, although vastly different in teaching and philosophy, all research seems to confirm that intricate order of things. We can sum it up this way: deeply held beliefs about yourself and life are expressed in the form of a purpose. Purpose, through your thoughts, leads a vision for your life. That vision now dictates your choices and actions, and from there your results are formed. We could call this your blueprint for life. It has been given many labels, but they are just that – labels. What matters is that you identify a clear and specific system that is beneficial for you.

First and foremost, beliefs and purpose are so dramatically important that we need to get a good understanding of what they are and how they influence your life. Here is an illustration of this concept that proceeds directly from the racing world. As you may already know, races take place around what we call "racing series": NASCAR, Indy, Formula 1, all the "Le Mans Series" – American, European, and the newer Asian Le Mans Series. Of all the Le Mans race-car types, the ultimate vehicle in sports-car racing is called a "Le Mans prototype" or LMP for short. You will never see it on the roads as it is a "race-only" vehicle, confined to exclusive use on race tracks. Prototypes are built for one thing only: racing and winning races. Many will be able to run up to 24 hours straight in full race conditions. These mighty endurance racing machines are purpose-built vehicles. There is only one function for them: dominating all of the other grand tourism classes and winning the overall race. They are extremely fast and yet must also be reliable and allow for major repairs executed at lightning speed while the race is in progress.

In October 2008, Scottish driver Alan McNish was piloting the #1 AUDI prototype called the "R10 TDI". The #1 Audi launched out on the track for the warm-up lap of one of the most important races of the year. It was wearing its #1 as series champion of the prior year. McNish was starting on the front row, having placed his car in second place during the qualifying round of the Atlanta, Georgia, "Petit Le Mans" 12-hour race. This legendary American race had attracted many major car manufacturers from all over the world. Peugeot was on pole position with his mighty rocket ship named the "Peugeot 908 HDI FAP". Peugeot's 908 had come from Europe after he had endured another painful defeat at the 24 hour of Le Mans with their state-of-the-art race machine. They were there to avenge their shortfall two months prior on the French country roads in front of 250,000 fans and millions of spectators worldwide tuning in to their TV for what is known as the greatest race in the world.

That day in Georgia, everything would count on the race track and in the pit lane for the next 12 hours solid. Huge sums of money and human resources are invested to showcase the supremacy of race drivers, teams, and technologies. Racing, for many decades, has been one of the most powerful marketing tools for OEM manufacturers: it is indeed a phenomenal image maker. For this reason, Peugeot does not want to kneel to Audi, and Audi will not back down to Peugeot.

The purpose-built Audi prototype, the epitome of the winning race car with a record-winning streak of eight consecutive victories at Road-Atlanta Grand Prix, is travelling downhill on turn three when suddenly the rear tires lose their grip, causing the back of the car to spin out of control. McNish, one of the greatest sports-car drivers in the world, cannot bring the car under control and he violently hits the tire barrier. The damage is severe. Understandably, McNish is in total disbelief but does not let his upset take the best of himself. He steers his Audi back onto the track; the car is limping back to the pit lane on three wheels with bad suspension damage a few minutes away from the start. That is one of the most upsetting positions in which a world-class driver could be—making a little driving error on cold tires at slow speed. Even though it is only one small mistake, that small mistake can have grave consequences. In a race in which every tenth of a second counts, the car is now back in the garage just before the start. Evidently, this incident is likely to terminate the chances of Audi scoring another victory despite many days of meticulous preparation.

The Audi team was about to demonstrate that morning what they are famous for: preparedness and responsiveness. They performed what seemed virtually impossible. The damaged Audi R10 was back on track in a matter of minutes, with replaced suspension, brakes, wheels, and all damaged body work. Alan McNish rejoined the race with only two laps down from his competition, and excitement was at its highest!

After a superb piece of driving, Alan McNish and his co-driver Dindo Cappello, the AUDI R10 TDI, crossed the finish line in first position as the fireworks erupted over the track and into the night skies. This was an outstanding display of talent, endurance, persistence, and total winning attitude onboard a purpose-built vehicle that had been able to rebound from its most devastating moments.

"Le Mans prototype" power can be brought into your life when you "purpose shift". You will unleash enormous power that comes from your heart's desire, and you will express the unswerving commitment and diligence to achieve your chief goal in life. As you gaze at the beauty of the winning race car, you must know that this prototype did not appear out of nowhere. A manufacturer made a decision to build it; his will and thoughts became reality, and many people contributed their motivation and energy to build only the best. Likewise, your life will shift away from an average level of performance to a high-performance level of your own design. Like "Le Mans prototype" team and drivers, you will have only one mission: race at your highest level and win.

When obstacles come to destroy your goals, hopes, or aspirations, as they did for Audi on that morning, you will be able to get back into the race quicker than you think is possible. Audi could perform this outstanding task because the structural integrity of the high-tech carbon fibre cell was not damaged at all – it had perfectly sustained the high impact. Had this underlying structure been compromised, the outcome would have been disastrous and final. This same resilience will apply to you when your resolve strengthens and when you are in pursuit of your life's heart desires. You will be able to perform lightning fast repairs and re-enter the race of life and ultimately see that chequered flag waved in front of you, although for a moment it might have seemed as though all was lost.

You must "purpose shift" away from the status quo of a life by default and choose to stop travelling the path of luck and chance. You can choose to become transformed by the renewing of your mind as you tap into your very own "purpose shifting".

Purpose shifting does not have to happen all at once, or in a single area. True purpose shifting will cause a chain reaction and will affect all areas of your life. It certainly has caused me to become more alert as I decided to engage high performance in my life. All that is dear to me is involved in this: my relationship to my wife and my children, my career, my finances, my contribution to society, even to my health and fitness level, without even discussing the subject of spiritual growth, which is inevitably part of the process in some way.

I purpose shifted the day I made the decision to live out the life I was born to live. No more compromise, fears, and limitations. Although these enemies of true life could not all fully disappear at once, I decided that I was the one responsible for the way I feel, think, and act – I was going to live my life with "Le Mans prototype" preeminent determination to become all that I could be.

RACE ENGINE

CHAPTER 7

At the heart of a "Le Mans prototype" (LMP) design is a powerful power plant that is a marvel of engineering in itself and the object of huge developmental efforts and costs. The power plant in a LMP1 can develop around 700 hp and over 800 ft-lbs of torque; for an LMP2, it is about 500 hp and around 300 ft-lbs. Top speeds can be in excess of 220 mph – not exactly your average road car performance! The primary role of the race engine is not to excite the race public with the screaming sound but to create as much forward motion as possible in straight and cornering conditions. It is a lot more than raw horsepower. Contrary to the popular belief, power and speed are not necessarily the same.

Many of us have been programmed since childhood to believe that some "horsepower factors" in our lives will result in desired outcomes and allow us to live the good life. As such, formal education and specialisation in a trendy industry field are promoted as the ultimate ticket to professional success. As adults find out later in life, reality sends a slightly different message, with only less than 50 per cent of the population feeling satisfied about their work and only 20 per cent expressing passion for their line of work. What happened to the other 80 per cent? With education, you will hopefully have a decent salary, be able to finance a decent lifestyle, and take care of your family. All of that is great, but discontent is still overwhelmingly present for so many people who want the reassurance that there is more to life than the rat race, feeding the economic system. You may be one of these people who still feel like something is missing.

You may realise today that raw horsepower gives you societal security but still leaves you with a lack of traction when it comes to a sense of fulfilment.

When a race engine is designed, it will be both cause and effect. Its specifications are carefully directed to influence the big picture of the race car, and its effects will bring everything to life when the time comes to rev up the engine. For a person, the power plant is the mind, and it means that the type of thoughts you carefully craft in your life will influence all other elements of your life. The careful and precise specifications of each and every one of your thoughts will influence the overall design of the other areas of your prototype life. It will determine the horsepower of your life vehicle and the torque that it will deliver to move things forward.

If you want to change your life to a purpose-built wining prototype, you must start by changing your power plant, your train of thought, into something supportive of what you want to accomplish.

At the time I decided to respond to my racer-oriented success DNA and to start building our racing future, my son Joshua was only 10 years old. Beside the inarguable fact that we have a thirty year age difference, there were countless issues that could have defeated my initial decision. Not enough time, not enough money, too much uncertainty, all kinds of compromises to make. I had to use the power plant of my thinking engine according to my clear objectives and values. I had to screen my thoughts and reject those that would not help me take the proper action in the progressive realisation of our ideal. In all honesty, this process is far from over; on the contrary, it is being strengthened to address greater challenges as our racing and business agenda keep on gaining momentum.

You will need to learn the skill of disciplined thinking: staying focused on your desired results. A thought that proceeds directly from your heart cannot be easily diverted off course. Fantasies, daydreaming, or circumstantial thoughts, however, are unstable and dictated by impulses or conditions of the moment. You may not be used to thinking at heart level. However, you will soon realise that as you progress beyond logic to purpose, your thoughts are going to become clearer, more stable, and always ready to power up your journey to true success even in difficult times. When you live a life of superficial thoughts, you are very vulnerable and will usually get exactly what you fear. When you focus your energy on not losing, guess what will probably happen? You will get what you were focusing on. When you think at heart level, you do not throw logic away, but you power it with something of greater nobility which will increase your own power to stay on track…

CHANGE OF GEARS

CHAPTER 8

When was the last time you started driving your car in 5th gear? As most of you drive an automatic, you don't even think about it, as it is done for you. For those who drive a stick shift, you know better and would never attempt starting in even 2nd or 3rd gear without severe stress on the engine and the transmission. The point here is that we all know that improper gear selection would result in a complete stall of the engine. Gear selection is critical to running your life race properly. You instinctively recognise that you cannot afford to miss out or stay in first gear if you want to accelerate your results.

Everything in the world is first born, then it grows and develops. God in his wisdom has given everything in life a progression, from the most humble stages of life to the most impressive achievements.

When you come to grips with your heart's desire, engage your unique talents, and decide to move forward, you engage the first gear. Congratulations! You are moving forward; the movement is noticeable, and that is enough to get you pretty excited. I personally experienced that very situation when I decided to ask to meet with a renowned American driver named Terry Borcheller.

Terry is a very successful sports-car race driver; he competed several times at the 24 hour of Le Mans (3rd in GT1), American Le Mans Series (2003 GTS Champion), and in Rolex Grand-Am GT and Daytona prototypes to name a few. His most recent success is the overall win of the 2010 Daytona 24 hour, ahead of the most talented drivers in America, including Jimmy Johnson, Helio Castroneves, Ryan Hunter Ray, Jun

Pablo Montoya, Scott Pruett, and others. He did not achieve this result by himself alone; it was the result of a phenomenal team effort with Auto Express Racing and the other co-drivers. You will meet Terry later in this book, as he granted us an interview to contribute to this work and give you his personal approach on creating success in racing and life.

Prior to that meeting, which took place at the Mosport Grand Prix of Canada of the ALMS, all I had were fairly vague and unrefined thoughts and feelings about moving into professional racing. After Terry generously granted me 45 minutes of his time, I left with some more precise knowledge and understanding and a complete racing development plan in which I am living right now. After that meeting, it became clear to me that I could engage the first gear. You cannot be in first gear without specific knowledge and a specific plan to execute. But I still had to make the decision to follow through.

I was now equipped with essential knowledge; to my surprise at the time, Karting was going to be a major development step. I had very limited knowledge about Karting. I had seen fun go-karts for kids in amusement parks but not much else. I had heard that many "star" drivers had grown through Karting, including Michael Schumacher (seven-time Formula 1 World Champion), but never guessed the significance of this stepping stone. It made sense that my nine-year-old son would take the Karting route, but I had a hard time conceiving that it was what I needed. Indeed, Karting is a serious racing development tool, and my ability to perform in Karting would become a strong indicator towards racing more powerful race cars in the future. I took on Terry's viewpoint, as I believe that advice from mentors is not to be argued with but applied.

I still struggled with the thought that I could start my racing development path by being beat by teenagers. That would be horribly humiliating. Maybe it would kill my vision from the get-go. The real question remained: did I want it bad enough? At that time, my son Joshua developed a surprisingly mature and highly motivated racing vision for himself. I will never forget the day when my little 9 year old uttered profound words as he stopped in front of Penske Racing's trailer. Staring at the yellow Porsche Prototype RS Spyders, Joshua called me over and said "Daddy, I don't know what it is, but there is something in me that is telling me that one day I will be driving one of these." He was not fantasising but witnessing the early and unhindered indicator of part of his life's calling. Now that Joshua had responded to this early calling, we had to develop two drivers simultaneously! Not an easy task... My own vision had suddenly expanded to a greater dimension, which was triggering destiny in my own son's life! Since he was committed himself, we were now upgrading my own vision to a larger one to encompass Joshua's vision. It took a little time, money, and logistics, but we made a decision in 2007 to launch Amaris Racing (www.amarisracing.com) with the ultimate aim to race in the ALMS and the 24 hour of Le Mans by 2015. A couple of years later, at age 14, Joshua has confirmed his strong talent, affirmed and matured his motivation and is well on his way – the dream is now becoming increasingly real! It may be vulnerable, but it is surely gaining momentum, moving inexorably forward.

Gear one had been revved up, and we engaged gear two: a full season of racing with our own race vehicles. As we started building our race team and hit the track for our first serious races, Joshua and I were in for a surprise. We had no idea of the complexity involved with setting up these race karts at a competitive level. Setting them up for fun can be quite simple, but to win against high level competition it is a whole other world! Terry's advice was proving right on the money. We would have to learn not only about race driving but about the whole, detailed universe of chassis setup and engine performance, race strategy, rules and regulations, and many other things. This created more upshifting and acceleration, and it became really exciting and rewarding.

At the time of this writing, the acceleration is becoming more exponential, causing my whole life to shift to new levels of demands to deliver high performance. It is both exciting and frightening. My whole life is now upshifting so quickly that I find myself trying to keep up. But as a racer, I should not be surprised by high speed and all that goes with it. After all, I need to keep my eyes on the track towards the finish line, and that is a wonderful feeling.

As you learn to "upshift" again and again by making fast and faster decisions, you may find yourself walking with the ground forming under your feet as you walk. At that point, faith and vision are a must. Faith speed is the ultimate speed as you make decisions based on a lot more than what you think is possible. Famous billionaire businessman Richard Branson still makes these kinds of decisions every day as chairman of the Virgin Group. According to him, if his guts say yes, he is going for it. You and I are not at his level yet, but as you start upshifting, you will be amazed at the velocity you can gain. You will be surprised to be part of new social groups and to form new friendships and partnerships. Your whole life will be vibrant and alive with inspiration, vision, and brand-new levels of achievements.

FACETS OF SPEED

CHAPTER 9

Lap times in racing conditions are made of pure forward speed. They reflect the combination of all track factors, including traffic and asphalt conditions. The final average speed with all these factors is what wins it. No sane race driver would ever drive pedal to the metal all the time. Therefore, no one should feel guilty of not progressing at top speed all the time.

Although this book is mainly about personal development, it is important to understand that true self-development is not only about you, by you and for you. You may now say, "Well, I am confused; I thought I had all this power to make things happen." Well, yes, you do, but you should be equally aware of how dependent you are on those around you. By dependence, I do not mean being a slave of anything; I am simply referring to the acknowledgement that life is much bigger than you, and that we are all interdependent on one another. Relax; stop controlling everything. Life in this world is too big to even dream that you can control it all. Somehow we know that, but we still go on trying to force our way, and in doing so, we too often create long-term damage in return for short-term reward.

We should never desire to drive pedal to the metal all the time in our lives; many who have done this have nearly destroyed themselves emotionally, physically, and even spiritually. This is life abuse, which is only too often mistaken for the true speed of success.

Le Mans prototypes, as in aviation, make use of a "pitot tube" (device named after its inventor, Henri Pitot) and other measuring devices in order to have the most accurate measurement of their speed. However, when it is all said and done, the fancy equipment is not what draws the line in the sand – it is the clock that gives the verdict and settles what the true racing speed really is. In qualifying, true race speed is called qualifying time. In race condition, true race speed becomes a product of many factors, including pit stop, refuelling, tire change, and even driver change in ALMS and other endurance racing series, and off-course traffic on the race course.

The winner is the one who is fastest overall, taking into account all of the factors that make up the racing environment. Some drivers can be better at qualifying than racing and vice versa, and of course some are great in both conditions.

In order to reach life's goals, we first want to be sure that we have a clear understanding of our final and complete aim – not just some fraction of it. Our heart's desire exists in the context of our lives at large. Before determining the fastest speed to get there, we have to consider all factors at play. Also, at times we will have to stop in the pits in order to regenerate ourselves and get some fuel and tire changes. We then want to know the conditions of our "life track" and adjust our speed accordingly.

As everyone knows, it takes a severe toll on your performance when you get off track, trying to push too hard. Your relationships, your spouse, your family, or your health may be damaged, and it could take you longer to repair them than if you had gone at the proper speed, with the proper integration of all factors.

As for myself, I was amazed and relieved to realise that the crucial aspect of my "complete success picture" – having high-quality relationships with my children – could be nurtured within the perimeter of my racing endeavours. My son wanted to race with Dad but had to prove that he had the talent, the determination, and the proper attitude to move forward, and he does. His recent 3rd place finish in his class at the 2009 Canadian Karting nationals proves it. I have been able to take all of that racing that has birthed in our family life and expand the dynamics of success to my young daughters.

Strategise your race; know specifically what you are aiming for. Remember to take into account all race factors and leave nothing out; otherwise, it could come back to damage your final results. Build towards your ideal with the "total speed" concept at the forefront of your thinking. Never forget to brake before the next corner in order to adapt your life or business racing speed. Manage your race well, and you will be successful, even as you cross the finish line…

RACING ALLIES

CHAPTER 10

Allies: just the sound of it is comforting, isn't it? In motor racing to beat the competition, you need a great team that has great team members, race drivers of superior talent, attitude, and commitment, and a race car of superior performance. Technology may change, rules will vary, but the fundamentals don't change. You can never race successfully in an antagonistic environment; you need people to believe in you. You need allies who will support you when things go wrong, or favour you and promote you when your hour has come. These allies can be in your own team, in your family, among your friends, or they can be found even in other teams. As we pursue high-performance life and business, we instinctively know that we need circumstances and people to assist us in ways that we cannot help ourselves. Call it a lucky break, call it timing or chance, if you will. But the question remains: is there something that you and I can do to maximise the odds in our favour?

There are two powerful allies that I would like to introduce you to. They are called Wisdom and Understanding. I purposely capitalise the letters out of respect for these giant pillars of fullness of success. Wisdom is the ultimate and complete knowledge that applies to any particular matter, and Understanding is the processing of that wisdom in a form that serves a beneficial result.

A few thousand years ago, a famous king by the name of Solomon became the symbol of wisdom for ages to come. His net worth was of staggering proportions, approaching a trillion dollars in today's value – yes, that is trillion with a T! His annual base salary in gold alone was about $700 million or 22,000 kilograms of pure gold. His influence extended to other nations whose kings envied Solomon's insight in many matters of life and politics. They travelled long distances to learn from him, offering him outrageous sums of money in the form of lavish gifts just to get a glimpse of Solomon's wisdom and understanding. In today's world, he would certainly not only be the richest man, but the wisest and most extraordinarily paid success consultant you would ever dream of. If anyone ever tells you that financial wealth is solely dependent on the economy or technology, send him to Solomon for a "thinking check". Solomon would probably have been a great sponsor for my race team, Amaris Racing. He certainly had the means to invest, and I would have loved to race an ALMS prototype with the words Wisdom and Understanding written on it.

Solomon wrote in the book of Proverbs: **"Wisdom is better than gold and understanding better than choice silver" (Prov. 16:16)**. What a change of perspective from what most people believe! I repeat… Wisdom and Understanding are more valuable to you than gold and silver. This indicates where the cause is and what the effect might be: **Wisdom is not the effect of financial wealth; it is the root cause of it.** The converse also points to the fact that the lack of wisdom will lead to a lack of finances.

In pursuit of riches, we have stopped pursuing wisdom and, sadly, we pay the price for it. Imagine how life would be if seeking wisdom were a total commitment and determined pursuit. Don't you think that many problems would be met with prompt and powerful solutions?

Want to know more of the wisdom effect? Want to be mentored not by a millionaire, not by a billionaire, but by a trillionaire? Listen to these golden words of Solomon in Proverbs 8:11: *"Wisdom is more precious than rubies; nothing you desire can compare with her. Long life is in her right hand; in her left hand are riches and honour. Her ways are pleasant ways, and all her paths are peace."* Definitely some secrets of high-performance life in here.

If you want to tackle the real big stuff in life and you want high-performance living, take a moment to stop in the house of wisdom and listen to its advice before you go your own way. If you do, you will become, like others before you, one of the most prepared "life drivers" who ever walked the earth, not on your own merit, but on the merit of a superior power that will fuel your race to a staggering level. It will leave nothing untouched or unchanged; it will bring satisfaction in all areas of your life and will never leave you with the bitter taste of regret.

In case you are concerned that these things are invisible in nature and that you may miss out, look at it from an "effect" perspective. Not everything that we use in our lives is visible or can be easily explained. Likewise, think about this: the laws of aerodynamics were there before race cars were even conceived. These laws are supreme, immovable, and are not affected by the intervention of men – they just are. Can you see air flow and aerodynamics? Not unless you use some advanced equipment; however, you can perceive the effect and adjust it to your desired results! The reason we have managed to produce faster and more efficient race cars today is simply because we are developing a better understanding of how to use them. We have learned to use them so well that at around 120 mph, a high-level performance prototype could drive completely upside down because of the effect of generated down force. Down force is meant to increase aerodynamic pressure on the car in order to increase tire grip and turn speed. When did we invent down force? Never! It has always been there as one of the multiple facets of aerodynamics. It was there always, but we did not see it until someone had the wisdom to put it into form. Such a man was Jim Hall with his Chaparral race cars, in the 1960s. Their use of the laws of aerodynamics gave them an enormous competitive advantage. Today aerodynamics has become the battleground for victory as much as engine and chassis have, and yet for a long time no one had learned to use this invisible power.

In the same way, the "laws of life" are our racing allies as we learn what they are and how to work with them. No need for fancy inventions. You actually have powerful agents right now, ready to assist you in your quest: their names are Wisdom and Understanding. I know we don't hear of them very often in the news or in job requirements. Yet these forces attached to the human heart and mind can power your quest to new levels of performance with joy and fulfilment. Literally everything in your own life and business can be affected by the diligent pursuit and application of Wisdom and Understanding. They are your allies; use them. And please do not be afraid to ask God for a lot; it does not cost any money. There is no limited supply, no side effects, only alignment with the essence of life itself. I will concede that, since you cannot download Wisdom and Understanding with your USB stick, it may take a little searching, but if as a starting point you read the book of Proverbs and start applying what it says, it will not be long before your results start showing the difference…

COMFORT TO PERFORMANCE

CHAPTER 11

One major choice you will have to make is to accept that comfort and great speed seldom go together. A Le Mans prototype is no exception to that. The truth of the matter lies in the fact that the chassis is built for high performance and is equipped with very stiff suspensions. In 2009 at Sebring International in Florida (one of the most famous road courses in America, which welcomes the Mobil One Grand Prix of the ALMS every year), veteran Audi driver Marco Werner suffered a severely bruised rib due to the repeated impact of his prototype on the bumpy race track. I remember seeing another driver wear Karting rib protectors. I am sure that you have driven on bumpy roads before, but I doubt that you have ever damaged your ribs; at least I hope you haven't. When you see a prototype cornering turns one and two of Mosport International in Canada, you witness something pretty special that defies the imagination; the car stays on the track at such high speed, even in plunging blind corners. Yet this is the reality of those drivers and cars that venture into extraordinary domains of speed without necessarily looking for trouble.

Although of a different league, a race kart will expose similar characteristics, albeit in a much lower envelope of speed it will still impose on the racer two to three "Gs" of cornering force. These forces can be a real deterrent for the uninitiated driver. I remember bringing one of our sponsors to the race track after the racing season. Per his confession, he had a lot of fun, but he endured a lot of pain even though he was in good physical shape. He was simply not accustomed to these forces. With several "Gs" of lateral acceleration, you become very aware of the weight of your head. LMP prototype will push up to four "Gs" of lateral acceleration – as much as a fighter pilot might experience. These are enormous forces by all accounts. As previously explained, race karts are on the lower end of the racing spectrum only in size. When it comes to racing exercise for the driver, they take on a different aspect. My point in mentioning this aspect of race karts is to tell you that you can start with smaller dimensions of your final desires, whatever it may be. Then, step by step, you will experience the progressive realisation of your objectives following the principles discussed in this book. Too often, we don't start because we want all or nothing and deprive ourselves of the growth path on the way towards our achievements.

I am here to tell you that whether you are looking at implementing change in your company, or change in your family, you can start harnessing these very same principles today that will carry you to the top – to the final results that you really want. Focus on learning the principles because they will unfailingly carry you to the top.

Only by changing your life philosophy to "purpose shifting", as previously disclosed, will you enter into a new awareness and start experiencing first-hand these life-acceleration principles. At that point, you will either choose to stay in the cockpit, putting up with the discomfort and the forces that challenge your neck muscles to keep your head on your shoulders or you will retreat into the comfort zone and find a reason why you cannot live the life of your dreams. However, if you are willing to embrace the discomfort of making life-changing decisions, you will also graduate to the front row of your race in life and business and will experience tremendous upshift in your life.

Here is another aspect of comfort versus performance. When you drive a race vehicle, you are looking for the limit of grip in every turn, acceleration, and braking phase. The only way for you to know where the limit of grip is, is through the feedback of your senses; your body will literally tell you what the car is doing. This happens so fast that you cannot think about it; you have to instinctively respond to what you feel from the car. The only way for you to feel that limit is to have stiffer suspensions, which will not only make the car more stable but also transmit more information to your senses. What may seem at first glance to be an inconvenience now proves essential to performance driving.

The same will apply as you set out to fulfil a life of great performance. You will feel uncomfortable at first. However, within a short time you will realise that this discomfort has activated new senses in your mind. You will now be able to perceive and feel things to which you were totally oblivious prior to making that decision to change. You will be alert, alive, and awake and able to pilot your life with much greater precision and effectiveness.

FAST OR COMFORTABLE? THE CHOICE IS YOURS.

PART 3
RACING LINES

DRIVING AND RACING

CHAPTER 12

So many times in life and business, we live only in a mere shadow of real freedom and don't really realise that there is so much more available. We are conditioned by our thinking to limit ourselves within very restrictive boundaries. There are no real limits to success; you are not breaking any regulations if you live with high performance and generate fast results. There are no speeding tickets. Yet we have become so accustomed to low performance that we start to think that little else is possible. By accepting the status quo of low-performance life or low-performance business, we run the risk of becoming either desensitised or immensely frustrated; in both cases, not a good choice. Desensitisation is a form of hopelessness, giving up on finding better solutions – such as accepting to be stuck in traffic every day without entertaining the idea that it could ever be different. Frustration is letting the daily traffic jam turn your thinking into anger, resentment, and impatience.

We could venture to say that we sort of have "life and business driver's licenses". What are they? The right to work and expect compensation, the right to trade in the form of goods and services and expect fair exchange, the right to make a profit. Frankly, all is fine so far; nothing is wrong with that, right? We also have the right to accumulate possessions, the right to build relationships, the right to find our place in society, along with many other rights. Our life and business driving skills are supposed to manifest themselves in satisfying results, and often they do. All of this is fine until we find ourselves possibly stuck in "life and business traffic jam", captive of life's daily demands; then we start to realise that what were once our fresh aspirations and hopes are now conditioned by the system around us. Sadly, we can easily neglect to use our creative and inborn abilities to live a life of greater dimension and freedom. That is where we risk resigning ourselves to our condition or experiencing tremendous frustrations with loads of negative consequences.

However, just keeping our thinking alive engages a whole new game and most likely will lead us to have greater control and influence – and therefore, much greater enjoyment in everything at home or at work. Bob Proctor, world renowned expert on personal development is called the "master thinker" by Doug Wead, Former special advisor to the president of the United States. Yet he was once an individual without direction, stuck in a low paying job as a firefighter earning $4,000 per year and owing $6,000. Bob Proctor, unstuck himself from the neglect of his true potential after understanding that anything which made his life was first made in his thoughts. Nowadays, Bob Proctor, is not only the chairman of Life Success group of companies, but he has touched the lives of millions of people and despite being in his seventies, is still vibrant with passion and energy to teach people all over the world about the power of their paradigms of thinking.

Don't think you have to start a company of your own to experience freedom and high-performance living at work. I once heard the story of a young man, let's call him Sam. Sam had Down syndrome, yet he became the success story of the town. How did he do it? He was a bagger at the grocery store. Not a glamorous place to start with – at first glance, that is. He was determined to make a difference for the clients of the store and used his own creativity to make it happen. Sam loved quotes; they motivated him, and he decided to share them with his customers. Before long, his checkout line ran right through the store, as Sam was placing the thought of the day into every grocery bag. People were not shopping anymore; they wanted to meet Sam! They were touched and blessed by Sam's simple yet significant initiative. He had stepped out of the traffic jam of boring work and into the race track of excellence in customer service. Sam did not choose to focus on what he had to do but rather on what he wanted to do. That inspired people, and Sam did it right where he was.

■ RACING STRATEGIES TO CREATE HIGH PERFORMANCE

You have to realise that all of the different types of decisions you make fall into two main categories: the "have to" decisions and the "want to" decisions. Let's call the first one a default decision, as it reflects simply what you think you have to do. The second kind, the "want to", is a performance-based decision that is rooted in purposeful choice. Since we are working on equipping you with life-racing skills and impossible speed, it is time to go on the track to have a look at what this means and how it will impact your results.

Are there default "have to" decisions that must conform to the demands of the race? Absolutely. Although racing is all about maximum speed, think about this: racing is also highly regulated. Infractions in the pit lane, for example, are penalised by drive-through penalties, meaning waiting in idle under the watchful eyes and slow-running clock of a race marshal while your competition is zooming on the track at race speed. That is pure torture for a racer in race mode, trust me! However, rules have a limited role, which is to promote fair play. Following the rules is about not losing time, but it will not give you a competitive edge. I have never seen a "Rules Champion", although sportsmanship is encouraged and occasionally recognised. If you want speed and high-performance results, you have to take on the "purposeful choice" to race to win, not just follow the rules by making "have to" decisions. Similarly, if you are just following the rules of the race of life and business, although they are important, they will not be enough to get you where you want to go – you have to learn to create speed in other areas by making "high-performance" choices. Being a good citizen and paying your taxes is important, and getting an education is important – but it is not enough to move you forward to realise the life you really want. Paying the bills is good, but your marriage might crave a whole different emotional dimension. Having a good business plan, good corporate policies, and a good marketing department are all important, but this is not high-performance stuff! These are only basic fundamentals, so don't get caught in dedicating all of your life or business energy to this. Make high-performance decisions and take high-performance actions by choosing which outcome you are really looking for; take the time to understand what it is that you and your entourage, your team, and your family really want to accomplish. Put some serious effort into understanding which kinds of results are desired before you forge ahead and start building.

The primary desired outcome of motor racing is clear – winning! "Wanting to compete and win" is the primary force that will provide the necessary direction and harmonious combination of talents and efforts for best performance. On the track, the racer who is in control of his racing machine will have to do more than make split-second decisions during the race; he will also have to learn to prepare himself before the race and choose which mindset he is going to operate with.

In his book *Drive to Win: The Essential Guide to Race Driving*, racing ace, engineer, and team manager Carol Smith says, *"The business of being a successful racing driver is very much a mental endeavour; in fact, after a reasonable amount of physical skills and racing experience has been deposited in one's personal bank account, achieving excellence as a racing driver is about 98 per cent cerebral and 2 per cent physical."* What a revealing statement! Ninety-eight per cent of the final edge of success is a mental fitness issue. Mental fitness comes through choosing to harness the power of supportive thinking – a form of thinking that supports the results we are looking for. Needless to say, complaining and arguing have no part in this. Do I choose to focus my attention, my emotions, and my energy to help me achieve my results, or do I let distractions and problems dictate how I feel and steer me away from what I am trying to accomplish? Mental fitness will act as a major force in deciding the outcome. It will have a much more conclusive effect than many so-called success factors like money, promotion, and opportunity will have.

Steven Covey frequently says, *"Our ultimate freedom is the right and power to decide how anybody or anything outside of ourselves will affect us."* Covey explains that the space of freedom is found between stimulus and response. It is not what happens to us that makes us or breaks us, but how we chose to respond to it. Personal freedom is directly related to personal responsibility. As I refer to personal responsibility, I am not thinking in terms of obligation but rather in terms of opportunity to influence everything that comes our way by accepting responsibility for our choices. I battled a long time with that concept, thinking that when

I was the victim of a given situation, I should not take responsibility for it. However, I quickly realised that this was a dangerous path, as it would leave me at that: just a victim. Victims do not win races. Only victors do! So, reluctantly, I started to consider where it would be healthy for me to accept constructive responsibility and start engaging my walk of life and business towards more powerful solutions. Frankly, at first it is not pleasant, but your newfound freedom quickly outweighs the cost. There is an ever-growing sense of freedom in the acceptance of constructive responsibility.

If you want to live life in prototype-racing mode, you must accept the responsibility that it will be all up to you. You cannot let the car drive you, or you will suffer the consequences. You must be in control, but before being in control of the car, you must be in control of your own heart and mind. As Carol Smith said earlier, it is 98 per cent mental, or internal, choices. The good news is that you have been given the enormous power of choosing how you want to live. You may feel overwhelmed at first in realising that you have not practiced this or forgot it for too long or used it too sparingly. You must choose to begin; get started or restarted or expand into more – but harness this power that was given to you in order to succeed in all that you do.

Everyday driving as well as everyday living life by default without desire, vision, or ambition of your own is both easy and destructive. It will leave undone all that makes your personality unique and will leave the path of life empty of your own marks and triumphs. Just like high-performance driving, living by choice is a risky venture; after all, you may fail at tackling your heart's desire even as you push the envelope of your life limits. Worse, you may go broke or may even be ridiculed by your peers. But one thing is for certain: you will never go back to where you started. That is a promise. How can I be so sure? Albert Einstein refers to the principle above: *The mind, once expanded to the dimensions of larger ideas, never returns to its original size.*

DECISION AND REFLECTION

CHAPTER 13

In trying to fit the world into our small boxes of assumptions, it is easy to end up with a crisis on our hands. We start to wonder why our teenager (or spouse, or boss, or employees) just doesn't get it. We forget that as we interact with people, we are dealing with an infinite variation of tastes, preferences, aptitudes, inclinations, and other variables. We like having everything our own way right now. We tend to resent it when things don't flow according to our expectations and timing. We are insecure when we do not feel totally in control, when we don't have the upper hand or the last word. We may even think that being a good leader is about being right all the time. This is a deadly trap in which we run out of true high-performance steam really fast. In right and wrong, good and bad, left and right, there is always a winner but also a loser – and nobody likes being a loser. That is why we need to readjust our approach.

If you doubt the importance of quality communications, let's hear from one of America's personal-development gurus, Anthony Robbins: ***The way we communicate with others and with ourselves ultimately determines the quality of our lives.***

Instead of you thinking about yourself as being right or being wrong, let's simply look at the results. Here is the question: what kind of results are you harvesting? Are you satisfied with your results in the sales field or in the boardroom, with your clients and prospects, with your competition? Deep inside of ourselves, you and I know that this "being right" and "being strong" approach will never really help us in building strong, lasting relationships with our children, with our spouses, with our business partners, or with our colleagues and clients.

Perhaps I am making you uncomfortable here, but I guess you know by now, since chapter two, that comfort and high performance don't go well together. Although it may be temporarily rewarding to have superior and dominating authority, we intuitively know that this in itself is simply not the best that we can offer. Suit up and let's go on the track. Let's go get a feel for it from the race car and get some understanding for optimal "race results" for yourself and your team.

As you now know, racing is a multifaceted endeavour: you are racing a race car with its own complexities, on a race track with its own particularities, and competing against a field of other highly motivated racers who want the very same thing that you want.

The first thing that a racer knows is that no one wins all the time. Who would watch a race series if the same driver were to win over and over without exception? Second, the experienced driver, although constantly racing to be at the front, will also display an uncanny ability to monitor his environment and will take into account the strengths and weaknesses of others in order to achieve his aim. It is so much more of a cold calculation than a demonstration of awareness and alertness to be engaged in the whole game, not just a segregated part. The driver's race team will help him in finalising this live race strategy so that opportunities can be seized by adequate choice and timing of a pit stop, refuelling, and tire change.

Roger Penske of Penske Racing, referred to as the "Captain", is one of the world's most renowned racing personalities and an outstanding racing strategist. The accomplished billionaire businessman started as a successful racer to become chairman of the Penske Group, which owns many companies, including the famed Penske Racing Team. When Roger is in town, everyone knows that he is there to win, as he demonstrated in 2009 at the Indianapolis 500 with another victory – this time with Brazilian driver Helio Castroneves at the wheel.

For most people, when you make a turn, you simply turn the wheel where the road is going – end of story. And if you are racing? Are you just doing the same thing, only faster? Well, the answer here is no. As racers, we entirely depend on the race track design and conditions. Our interpretation of the track is so important that some racers even take time to walk all or at least parts of it. What happens here is that the nature or design of the turns and their associated curbing will determine the most efficient way to negotiate it. When it comes to awareness of your racing environment, you must absolutely know how to read your corners. You have to discern if you are dealing with an entry corner or an exit corner, also referred to early or late apex corner.

For the purpose of this book, I will call these life turns: I invite you to view them, respectively, as the decision corner and the reflection corner. Now, let's go back on track.

DECISION CORNERS/ENTRY CORNERS

At times, life requires making decisions at the snap of a finger. This will require that you seize opportunities that come your way by acting now. There will be little time to think, and a great deal of confidence will be needed to make a decision. I recently faced such a time, when presented with the opportunity to publish this book. I had not planned to publish anything in the near future; frankly, no book at all was on my radar screen. When a certain set of favourable circumstances on behalf of my publisher came together, l had to make a fast decision, although as you can image, writing a book is a rather time-consuming activity and definitely a schedule-altering one. I had to reprioritize several business items in order to accommodate this possibility, but I did it promptly without thinking for hours on end about the pros and cons. When you are in an entry corner, you cannot afford to handle it like an exit corner – you must accelerate immediately. When you are in an entry life corner, you also have to accept that overcoming your fear barriers, your doubts, and uncertainty is simply a strategic choice. It is suited to the moment, and you will reap the benefit once the turn is completed. Is it uncomfortable? Most likely. Like any direction change, it creates stress on the chassis on the race car; changing your life will create stress on you. But it is a creative stress, not a destructive stress. Although at times the significance of the change may make you feel like it is negative, in the end it will not be. Creative stress is still stress, but it will produce beautiful end results.

More often than not, we will resist the stress of rapid change and focus on the cost rather than the prize. That can be a big mistake, as by the time the opportunity passes you by, you will have to accept that you have missed it. Do not let that happen to you; master the art of negotiating "Life Entry Corners" promptly, relying on your heart and mind. When an opportunity comes around and you assess that it is in line with your true heart's desire and with your vision and goals, don't run the risk of missing it: take action swiftly.

REFLECTION CORNERS/EXIT CORNERS

On the other hand, there is another type of decision that can be characterised by quite the opposite: patience and analysis. This is the very definition of an exit corner: don't hurry, hold back a little and prepare for the exit, never yield to impatience. In an exit corner on the race track, it is all about preparing that reacceleration on exit. You must resist the urge to accelerate too early for fear of destabilising your vehicle, which will result in loss of grip, lack of acceleration, and loss of precious time in your race. In your life and in your business, you must know if you are in a reflection corner and not make the mistake of a hasty decision.

Perhaps you don't have the needed confidence, or the timing is off or there is excessive risk – all these factors must be evaluated. But understand that the extra time is spent on evaluation, not the decision itself. It could be in anything like starting a new career, starting a business acquisition, accepting new professional responsibilities, buying a new house, or going on the world tour of a lifetime.

In a reflection corner, don't be shy about adding time to the decision making. You must wait until you know that you can accelerate again as you make your decision. Interestingly, at first glance a reflection corner can look just like an entry corner. How do you tell the difference? Think in terms of outcome; will it benefit me to take a slow and methodical approach in delayed gratification or should I act now? Unlike on a race track, you may not have been there before, and you may not be able to afford testing sessions. So focus on developing your judgement and sharpening your senses. This will certainly be an exercise in discernment. The more you become used to it, the better your decisions become and the more your quality of results starts to improve.

Once again you will end up racing yourself first in this corner; the urge of impatience will want to have its say, but you will learn to stay in control. Never fall short of listening to the more truthful voice speaking inside of you, often referred to as the proverbial gut feeling. You may not be used to this and think that this inside stuff is for weak people, yet I challenge you to go for a test drive and let me know what you think of the results. Don't think that you will master this overnight; like race driving, it takes skills, but the payoff is huge. If you take the time and honour the design of the reflection corner, you will find it a friend who helps you make the right decisions at the right time for the right reasons.

COMMITMENT TO HIGH PERFORMANCE

CHAPTER 14

Since LM prototypes and airplanes both make extensive use of aerodynamic laws, I want to tell you a story that will take us to the air for a few moments. Some years ago, I took my first flying lesson, and it was an extraordinary moment. For the first time, I sat in the captain's seat. I was not holding the controls yet; my instructor was, which obviously explains why I am still alive to write this book! Once at an altitude of about 3,500 feet, I was given the controls of the low-wing, single-engine Socata Rally. There was not much to do, as the main objective was to become familiar with the controls and just not upset the aircraft. As it went well, my instructor asked me to do some low-bank turns. Hey, I thought that stuff was pretty easy! Well, with the next lesson, we started to tackle some more demanding manoeuvres, and soon I had to handle all of the parameters: altitude, attitude, speed, position, direction, navigation, and radio communications. Add to this an unstable air mass, and you can quickly have a handful.

I am sharing this with you to make a simple yet important point: adding new dimensions of control to your life will require greater learning and coordination. What you may assume is obvious from the ground is not obvious in the cockpit of an aircraft and requires extensive training and proficiency to stay safe. A high-performance life or business is like driving at racing speed, or like flying airplanes; it is a wonderful experience that requires ongoing commitment in order to benefit from it. That is why racers need seat time and pilots need flight time and proficiency checks. You cannot just visit "High Performance Land" once in a while, hoping for some high-performance results. Once you embark towards the life of your heartfelt dreams, you will not be able live it out half-heartedly, temporarily, or on occasion. A high-performance life requires a commitment decision; it is literally a lifestyle. There is no trying or thinking that it may not work out; there is only intentional and committed doing.

As you are committed to high performance, you also need to know what to do to achieve it. American Le Mans prototypes have a very elaborate design to get the best results out of all forces at work (i.e., air resistance, down force, grip, air turbulence, friction, acceleration, vibration, braking). The aero design requires either extensive time in wind tunnels or very complex computer modelling. The Acura LMP1 prototype ARX-02A was entirely designed and wind tested through computer modelling, which is a stunning achievement by Nick Wirth of Wirth Research in England. The car was first driven on a driving simulator similar to an airliner simulator. Experienced drive, 2009 Le Mans 24 winner and American Le Mans series champion, David Brabham, took it to the simulated track to find the exact dynamic behaviour of his car, which was yet to be built. This astounding technology is possible because precise laws govern all that we do throughout the created universe, including highly advanced aerodynamics. We also marvel at the fact that our lives are run within equally precise laws that require our awareness and understanding. The precision and reliability of these laws will become your friends as you develop high performance and impossible speed.

To illustrate the point, let's explore the concept of the high-speed handling capability of a Le Mans prototype and associate it with developing our own high-performance capability.

When you search for new possibilities for yourself, these possibilities will be found in your increased knowledge of the laws of life, which can be referred to as metaphysics. These laws are as precise as the laws of physics observed in our visible and material world. Both the physical and metaphysical (meta meaning beyond) partake of the same master stroke of creation. So if you feel like your life is somewhat chaotic, we could say in a race analogy that it has a handling instability problem; don't panic! Find the adjustment point in the way that you think, look at, and handle this particular situation. By doing some race adjustments to the situation, adjusting it to your true desired outcome, and finding what causes the handling problem, you will realise that you have considerable influence over it, and not vice versa – unless you let your situation run you over. I have experienced countless handling issues in my rally racing, and when my son Joshua and I started kart racing, we found ourselves having to deal with countless handling issues of our race karts. We actually found it very rewarding to first learn the principles derived from the physical laws at work on our race karts, and then apply the solution, influencing our results to be competitive and win races. We started unaware and incompetent and progressively moved to competence and mastery – and there is still a long road ahead as the complexity of race vehicles increases.

The difference is that now we are not as concerned as we used to be, since we know the process of discovery towards new levels of performance. That is, of course, until we move up to our next scheduled level, IMSA Lites Prototypes, where a new cycle of growth and acceleration will begin. How exciting!

POINTS OF NO RETURN

CHAPTER 15

A point of no return sounds a little dramatic, but it is a very important component of race driving. In life and business, it refers to unique forms of decisions leaving us with only one alternative: moving forward.

Points of no return can be experienced as you drive through a track corner at maximum speed; when you approach the apex, you will find yourself at a point of no return. Your car is committed to the limit of its grip; you can change your line or speed to some degree, but you cannot hit the brakes and try to put yourself on the safe side or you will almost inevitably lose control of your vehicle. All of this happens as you are running on the edge of loss of control. At times it can be heart wrenching – that is where gutsy racers have an edge over the competition.

The same is true in significant decision making, which might be life- or business-altering. Once you make that big decision, there is only one way out: forward and at max speed. Once you are committed to high-performance life and business decisions to make a turn for a new chapter in your life or in your company, once you have made the decision to go for the life of your heart's desire, you will most likely not be able to touch the brakes without running the risk of a crash. Scary perspective, isn't it? Well, that is the point! Points of no return are not cute little features. They mean that you cannot give up without a very severe cost to yourself and those around you; therefore, you don't even think of giving up, and that very attitude is what gives you the power to succeed – this is literally your ticket to the finish line. If you think this is a little kamikaze, you have to remember that the alternative is pure loss. Most people only *try* to do things differently, rather than truly moving in the direction of their true desires. When things get ugly, they resist a little, then pack up and leave. All they have to do is dust off their clothes and resume life where they started – they have gone nowhere; they have failed their vision. When that happens, as you keep on failing by yielding to pressure, it gets harder and harder every time to get back up and try again – you cannot afford a mind folder full of failure stories telling you why you should not try anymore.

I do not mean to scare you. On the contrary, it is by creating your own points of no return that you will become unable to fail casually and will dramatically increase your chances to succeed – failure is not an option! There is so much density in this process that you are not taking a chance at failing, so it is going to work. You will feel a supreme force deep inside, moving you from action to action until you realise your goal and make your dream happen, because success is tied to total commitment, and total commitment will result in what you are looking for. No one said that it was going to be easy to function at high performance, but you know the alternative is little to no performance at all, as well as boredom and frustration.

If you are committed to live a life of high performance, life will return the corresponding effect in making things possible for you. Don't think for a minute that the race driver is the absolute master of his race. He is only the skilled manager of the forces at work. None of the race thrills would be possible without the laws that govern every part of our physical universe. Your responsibility in creating success for yourself is not in creating something that didn't exist before but in forming a new reality based on existing principles and systems already in place for you to use. You will get the results you want, not by pride, arrogance, or sheer willpower, but by learning to cooperate with life on the basis explained earlier in this book: understanding your true desires and walking them out with wisdom, understanding, and commitment. Later we will touch on a complete sequential method to allow you to turn your true desires from dream to completion. Now think how reassuring that is. All matters of possibilities are already in place, and all you have to do is learn to trust them and use them.

BOLDNESS VERSUS HESITANCY

CHAPTER 16

I used to think that people who really succeed in spectacular ways are extraordinarily gifted and smart, and yes, that is very true occasionally. We all have extraordinary gifts, although we may not be aware of it. It is my belief that a true desire, a genuine heart's desire, cannot exist without the pre-existence of the corresponding potential to achieve it. Now, follow me here, as you must become convinced of this if you are to accomplish your purpose. Frankly, I do not have absolute proof of what I am saying, yet I have experienced many times that if I am capable and become 100 per cent determined and committed to making something happen, it does. And if I fail to have this high level of fully engaged desire, I only get haphazard results. At the centre of the failure are not my abilities, but the lack of boldness in achieving the goal.

As we assume that you are committed to making successful changes in your life, the natural companion of commitment is boldness. Many times as a trainer and mentor, I was asked to work with individuals who had good intentions but were lacking determination and commitment to create the high performance in their business and reach their stated goals. These people were either inexperienced and unstable or seasoned but disillusioned. When you ask them to establish a clearly constructed approach to their sales results, they conclude: "Well, I hope it is going to work." Now if you listen carefully, they do not really hope but rather think that it would be nice if it were to work out. Sadly enough, the outcome is virtually guaranteed: it will not work. Hope that is a wish is not hope at all. Hope, when it comes from a true desire, is a powerful force, but when it is used as a substitute for a wish or a whim, it loses all of its virtuous ability to cause you to succeed. True hope is bold, committed, has a focus forward, does not understand compromise or going back, and is full of expectancy. It does not even depend on probabilities or results but simply has the profound conviction that everything will be done to see the desired results materialised.

Hesitancy has little to no place in racing at all. When you need to make a pass, you either do it or you don't. You may have waited for the right moment and may show patience, but hesitancy is connected to a constant entertaining in your mind that something could go wrong. You may be bold, and you might attempt and fail, and that's okay. But hesitancy, when it interferes with a committed, high-performance life environment, will inevitably result in precious time lost as the intensity of the pursuit is diminished. Hesitancy is a by-product of doubt and fear of negative outcomes. It feeds procrastination but will never feed success.

Arm yourself with boldness. Think about commitment to high-speed turns in your life decisions, and remember that this is a place for the bold – not for the hesitant.

HIGH-SPEED BLIND TURNS

CHAPTER 17

The Mosport International Speedway is nestled on a terrain elevation called the moraine, which runs 160 kms, crossing north of Toronto, Ontario, and ending shortly after Mosport International Raceway. This setting of a naturally convulsed terrain has allowed for a very unique track design with turns of legendary renown. The ten-turn, 2,543-mile track has hosted Formula 1 events in the past with preeminent drivers such as Jackie Stewart and Mario Andretti. John Surtees, the only driver who has been world champion on both two and four wheels, had a dramatic accident there with a Lola F1, which lost a wheel in turn one and almost ended his life, terminating his career. The crippled champion would race again against all odds, despite devastating injuries that would have condemned most people to a wheelchair for the rest of their life.

Mosport is a very inspiring track, but it can be frightening, particularly in turns two, four, and eight. For that reason, even some seasoned racers are not too keen on racing at Mosport. Turn eight entry comes at you at the end of the long stretch straight up the mountain, arriving at the crest of the climb at speeds around 300 km/hr for LMP prototypes. Turns two and four are of the family known as "fast blind corners". A blind corner refers to one that hides your driving line and only reveals it as you go into the turn. When that happens in street driving, this is no concern, but at speeds well over 200 km/hr on a race track, it becomes a different story. Turn two, in particular, plunges abruptly while turning to the left, sending you hurtling down the sharp hill. Amazingly, LMP prototypes handle this turn well at over 200 km/

hr and with high lateral g forces, using their enormous down force to prevent the car from taking off when the track plunges downward. All of that may sound scary, but it is first and foremost a challenging environment that provides huge rewards for the equipped, skilled, and prepared.

Have you ever felt that you were taking on a blind turn when making a decision? Have you ever felt challenged to embark on something that you do not understand fully and cannot even see in advance? All you know is that you have to get started and you will figure things out as you go.

People who are detail oriented and do not like improvising or surprises tend to be very uncomfortable with "blind life turns". However, most major decisions in our lives do not present us with a full picture of the finished result. If you knew ahead of time what marriage and family pressures were going to be like, would you engage yourself wholeheartedly to build it in the first place? I don't want to sound cynical, but sometimes it is good to be unprepared. Many times we say, "I know it is going to be tough," but we really don't know; we just guess. Anyway, where would the thrill of a new adventure be if you could see the finish line before you start?

I will never forget the day in June 2007 when I decided to join my son Joshua in kart racing to engage our parallel-driver development path – this decision would have a profound and wonderful effect on the closeness that Josh and I have developed in our relationship. So here we were, a 10-year-old and a 43-year-old, embarking on the same adventure, with common aspirations and common goals. As we hit the track for a private training session (remember, I had been out of racing for 20 years), my mind and my heart were going a lot faster than my go-kart. Part of me kept saying, "This is silly; I should not be here. People are going to laugh at me." At that moment, I arrived at turn six of the Mosport kart track, which is, you guessed it, a blind turn at the top of a hill that sends you flying towards the most technical part of the track. It was an "ah-ha" moment! I received a lesson in a flash as the pavement rolled under my wheels. I realized that this whole life and racing project was going to be just like that turn – a blind turn, and there was only one way to figure out what was going to be beyond that line of sight: keep on going no matter what. I have used that particular piece of understanding countless times in my career and family life as we keep on making decisions. That day, the track had a lesson ready to deliver to me, a major ingredient towards success. It is amazing what can happen when you are on route to your true desires' fulfilment; everything you need to know and do will become possible. I certainly never thought I would learn a life lesson from a race track until that day.

I am proud to say that Joshua and I won many of the races we engaged in that year, and the year after that we each locked a championship title in our respective classes – not bad for beginners. By now I had to reorganise my business to make time for training on and off the track. I hired more staff to support me with my clients and managed to realise my sales production in only two or three days per week. I was creating a new environment to allow the next section of my "life dream pavement" to unfold.

You may not be comfortable engaging in anything that involves blindness ahead of you. Yet I am sure that you will agree with me that more than once there has been no other choice available. Planning and preparation do not lose their place in this perspective, but your plan will not last much longer than your next turn. This is where you will have to develop the art of adaptability to thrive in the unfolding reality of fast blind life turns.

DRY AND WET LINES

CHAPTER 18

The dynamic behaviour of a car changes in the rain, and the grip on the track is outside of the normal lines when rain comes down. Life's slippery conditions, such as difficult economy, new directions, and new enterprise, cannot be approached with a pedal-to-the-metal attitude; they will be similar to what is called a "wet race line" as they require smoothness and adaptability.

Very high-grip track can hide to some degree the driving imperfections of a racer. However, when the rain starts to fall, a whole new game unfolds. Some drivers who are very comfortable on the dry track find themselves in a predicament and not able to deliver their best performance when the weather shifts. This very situation happened several times at the Le Mans, as the Peugeot prototype, which is better suited for dry conditions, has a hard time competing with the Audi car when the track becomes slippery. It is not just the car; it is also very much your personal ability to handle the new difficulties. Many things change: your visibility is reduced to virtually nothing, and you have race vehicles all around with hardly inches of separation, as well as gallons of water pouring on your helmet visor. The race lines that you have grown accustomed to using in the dry conditions stop working due to rubber build up, creating a slippery band under your wheels. Answer to that problem? Look for "uncommon lines", or wet racing lines. These lines do not work on normal dry days but can create a phenomenal advantage in the rain.

When things become tricky in your life and business conditions, such as when the economy is challenging your sales or your income or your company, you have to think differently. That is not the end of the world. That may be the opportunity to create a new one. Wet lines are available at any time on a race track and should be used for best results only when the conditions are suitable. In the same way, when you lose some grip on your life enterprise, you need to consider whether you might need to adapt yourself and your way of proceeding. Is it a change in management approach, a change in competitive positioning, or a change in perception that is needed? Do you need to change careers or review the way you communicate with your clientele in decline? Straight growth and opportunities are more like high-grip dry race lines; you just sink your teeth into them and you will get the results you want. Wet conditions, however, require more thinking and analysis, more subtle decisions. And yes, this is your hour to shine! More often than not, when it gets "wet", people lose their edge and their confidence, or they make bad mistakes and spin out of control.

Wet line considerations are needed when your relationships are at risk, when tension mounts in the home, when your teenager seems to get out of control. The answer is not in trying to force things – that would make everything worse and could destroy exactly what you are trying to create. Rather, you have to negotiate a more careful approach and most likely let go of your old controlling ways. It may be frustrating at first, but it will certainly become rewarding when you overcome the initial resistance to change.

Make the effort to master the art of "wet racing" and create unprecedented high performance in your results.

PART 4
RACING STRATEGY

GOING FOR GOLD

CHAPTER 19

In 2008, as I was standing by the Audi R10 TDI LMP1 prototype before the start of an ALMS Grand Prix, I was struck by several things. First, the imposing presence generated by the overall appearance of the race beast sitting only a couple inches off the ground. Then I was amazed at the sense of flow you gather from the car. It is designed to slice through the air, but also to provide extraordinary down force that can exceed 4,000 lbs at 200 mph just from aerodynamic effects in order to achieve greater speed through greater grip in the turns. The 600 hp V10 power plant delivers nearly 800 lbs of torque through its diesel fuel-injection technology and is totally hidden from view, giving the car an unassuming quietness to its appearance.

The same can be said of your life, your business, or your corporation. Your final results, your products, or services are the culmination of all that has been designed, built, and assembled. The real question is: "Is that convergence really happening, or happening enough?" Before answering the question, let's give it some definition. Convergence can have many definitions, depending on its field of application. Here we are referring to the combination of two or more distinct entities creating a definite synergy that delivers a powerful and specific result. Although on the prototype, the engine, the gearbox, the chassis, and the suspension are all distinct entities, they purposely converge to produce the overall performance. At the end, no one would say, "Look at the engine driving down the straights" or "Look at the suspension passing on turn two" or "Look at the tires that are accelerating up the hill." You will agree with me that it would sound rather strange to refer to anything other than the car and its driver. In the same way, individual components of life or company departments, although distinct, must have a clear sense of convergence in order to produce the final result that they want. In a company, we commonly identify this function as teamwork. I choose to call it the "convergence effect", as it applies to anything in life as much as it does to business, and it is a lot more encompassing than teamwork. The convergence effect can power your step, whether on a personal-development level or corporate-performance basis.

So where does that lead us in mapping out and constructing our success journey and accelerating our results with impossible speed? Family, health, relationships, business, and financial success are all closely tied together as they stem directly from who you are as a whole. You must view all of these components of your life as one big picture of your overall purpose. Occasionally, in the search for convergence, you may actually prune your life tree a little in order to maximise the areas that are truly important to you. When you do that, you will regain a sense of control and harmony that will surprise you. Trimming your activities or effort is not necessarily cancelling but rather revisiting your emotional involvement, in re-evaluating what it is that you are really after.

By spending less time looking for the glories of success and more time focused on the functions of success, we find more profound motivation to achieve only that which is important to us. That way we travel lighter, with more power endurance as we see ourselves satisfied as part of a winning team – versus being a winning part! Harry Truman gave us an interesting perspective on this, which can help to create more convergence and more success: *It is amazing what you can accomplish if you don't care who gets the credit.* Any race driver knows this all too well. Although he is the one celebrated, he is fully aware of the investments of others and will make sure to capitalise on the strengths of the team and take his teammates to the top with him.

Michael Schumacher, like all racers, has a strong ego, which causes him to hunt for the outright win at any price – this has even created some severe controversy on his racing style. However, as he entered the

Scuderia Ferrari in Formula 1, he realised that having a fast car on the track would mean having a cohesive and convergent team of mechanics working for him with passion and dedication. It could not be all about Michael. It did not come easily; he joined in 1996 but won his first title for them in 2000. From there, they won five times consecutively. They had to become like family, committed to the same outcome. They became masters of convergence: technically, in communications, in relationships, in engineering, in racing strategy, and in execution. Michael was not the greatest by himself; he became the greatest with a fully convergent team. His will to win and dominate on the race track was never set aside; it was powered up by his convergence mindset.

RACING PLAN

CHAPTER 20

Every race is only as good as its planning and preparation. The accepted truth here is that diligence in planning is directly proportional to your expectation of successful outcomes. However, before a plan can be established, the vision of that plan has to be clearly spelled out in order to be successful and effective.

Let's face it; people make plans for their lives and their businesses all the time, but they are only haphazardly successful. The reason for this is that success is not as simple as taking a few action steps and then getting the results you want. Why doesn't this work? Few realize that real success begins in the mind and is an integral part of achieving your desires. Saying that you want something and being totally engaged in achieving it are very different things. If you don't understand how your own mind works and how to really engage every part of yourself to get what you want, you will very likely continue to try but only have limited success.

STATE OF MIND

Whether we like it or not, the state of our lives is a direct reflection of the state of our mind. This may seem a little abrupt, yet I promise you that this contains great hope for your future! This implies that if you do not like your present condition or results, the changing point will occur precisely at mind level. As you change your state of mind, your way of thinking about a given situation, you will become able to condition the result in a way that you like and control. At this point, I want to emphasise that" mind" does not mean brain. The brain is the primary physical centre of thought processes, but the mind is not physical, not even visible. You cannot put someone's mind on a screen for others to look at! Your mind is of a spiritual dimension and refers to the very core of your being: who you are today. You can develop yourself, as your mind is not static. What it takes is to think differently and believe in a different way about your life or your business – thinking in creative terms. You will acquire new perspectives and a new understanding. Once again, ask yourself: what do I want? State it clearly and start taking control of the situation by taking constructive action. As a normal by-product, things will start to evolve and change for you. You will soon realise that the same process that led you to frustration is now going to lead you where you want to go: you have gained control of your mind, and you can now control the outcome. Just as a driver races a high-performance racing prototype, you will converge all of your thinking and actions in a precise direction and start accelerating towards the finish line!

What are the practical steps?

VISION

First, you must have a clear vision of your goal in order to start. You don't necessarily need to know how you will achieve your goal or what the steps will be, you just need to hold the picture of what it will be like to achieve it. You may not be comfortable seeing yourself in that new position, new promotion, new career or new role in life, or in this new level of achievement. However, you must form a compelling vision on the screen of your mind to be able to start acting purposefully. Failure to do so will inevitably lead to uncertainty and procrastination and will render your results very vulnerable to failure. This vision is literally the seed of your future outcome; it is very precious and not to be treated lightly.

You may think, what if I do not have any image in my mind of what I want to accomplish? Actually, you can easily define your tastes and preferences, and you probably have a little bit of an idea about your character traits (dynamic, reserved, inventive, protective, creative, etc.).

All of these attributes of your person exist today because of certain "pictures" or conceptions that you have of your life. They are referred to as self-image or self-concepts. If you think of yourself as action oriented, you are describing your self-concept, the way you see yourself, which results in wanting to get things done. If you think that you are more of an analytical person, you are also referring to an internal concept or the internal picture that you have of yourself. Therefore, it is safe to assume that no one is without a picture of their ideal results in life or in business, because you know through your likes and dislikes how things should look in order for you to be satisfied.

Simply expand on this and try to form more definite pictures of what you would like your life or business to look like and what you would look like in it. Don't contemplate things only; see yourself in them! Want a new house? See yourself in it! Want a new car – how would it feel to drive it? Want more fulfilment with your kids – what would that look like? What would you do? You want to start up this new venture? Describe to yourself how you would feel as a result? Use your imagination! No one is watching, no one will make fun of you if you fail.

If you are not familiar with the process, you may think: what the heck? How is this whole-picture business going to help me accelerate my results? Just like a race car, your speed does not come only by pressing down the accelerator; you will need a lot of converging elements to create speed – including a powerful engine. Think about defining your future in your mind, exploring in pictures your future is like adding a few cylinders to your engine and throwing in a turbo too! It is going to get more powerful; you are going to get excited when you start to see over and over the new you forming a new reality!

Note: I encourage you to learn more about self-concepts and visualisation with books like Maxwell Maltz's *Psycho-Cybernetics* or a recent work by John Assaraf: *The Answer*.

When a race driver is chasing a car in front of him, he does not have the final picture of the pass, as this will unfold in a split second at the time of passing. However, he hosts the motivational picture of the pass, translated into the desire and the effort of going after the opportunity even to the point of creating it. There is a shift that happens from a matter of "if" to a matter of "when". The "when" is now being actively tracked, pursued, and even created by the race driver. Armed with the motivational picture, he will probably succeed unless the skills of his opponent prove greater than his own.

CONTROLLED THINKING

The human mind has the ability to think at a phenomenal speed and the speed of thought is very contextual. In 2008 the American Psychological Association published a study named "Psychological Effect of Thought Acceleration". This study interestingly refers to "thought acceleration" and its effect on the mood of people and their creative condition: "We all have had experiences where we feel as though our minds are racing, or at least moving faster than usual. We might take advantage of this surge in mental activity to begin writing a book or developing a new theory." By correlating speed of thought, mood and creativity, this studies indicates that we can have a positive impact towards the results we are looking for by choosing "how we think" and "how we take advantage" of our thinking condition.

Imagine also the consequences of letting thoughts running wild and in unproductive ways. If you are dissatisfied, you are not only because of a certain set of circumstances. You have allowed these circumstances to form by thinking them into reality through repetition. Let's say you have a mess on your desk that you cannot seem to clean up; did the mess happen, or did it form one item at a time? You allowed your thinking to tolerate a progressive degeneration of your desk until it turned into what it now is. The more you think about how messy the desk is, the worse it gets, and it can really accelerate. At that point, make a decision that the desk will be clean. Direct your thoughts and actions to create a new environment. Become creative and decisive, and start taking action right away. Think of how great you feel when the desk is clean, and regain control of the situation.

As companies understand and accept that the source of their own messes or successes are formed first in the mind of their executives and employees, they will invest more into helping people become aware of the importance of thought processes and learning how to manage it. Needless to say, desks are only the very tip of the iceberg. Sending junk emails or filling our mind with filthy material cannot be without consequences. Remember that there are always two sides to a coin, and you have to choose which one to look at, as you cannot view both simultaneously. Positive wholesome thinking and supportive focus and action will build results. Conversely, feeding our minds with negative and non-supportive input will slow down, decrease, and pollute your desired results – not to mention take your joy and peace away. By choosing to select what we allow in our minds, we create a tremendous rate of acceleration. By creating a dominant, wholesome picture of what we are building, we experience an increased measure of well-being. Any company that can give its employees understanding of this will create millions of dollars in productivity while lessening the pain of leadership. Effectiveness is first a mindset, a de-cluttering of the mind and restructuring of positive results as previously explained, through vision and goals. You have to start first at the root of the problem – the mindset.

The vision that you hold in your mind will form its corresponding reality. Beware, as this is not discriminatory of either good or bad. This mechanism will deliver with any intention you attach to it. Good outcomes and negative outcomes will proceed directly from your internal management. Your primary visions will give birth to feelings, and once the feelings are unleashed, be prepared – it will become very hard to put them to rest. So you had better make sure that it is what you truly want to pursue before you actually pursue it. The ancient king Solomon, whom we met earlier in this book and whose achievements and wealth were of impossible proportion, once said, *Guard your heart for it is the wellspring of life* (Prov. 4:23). Indeed, guarding our mind from the things that we do not want, and feeding them with the things that we do want, is vital to experiencing total-result acceleration.

Any skilled race driver will tell you that when a crash occurs on the race track, the last thing you want to do is look at the obstacles swirling in front of you. If you do, you will inevitably end up hitting them. In the case of a high-speed crash, the only way to escape is to look for the solution and disengage your mind from the problem, because what you allow your mind to focus on is where you will go. Amelia Earhart once said, "To worry is to add another danger." Worry is another form of a negative vision expecting problems, which distracts you from looking for solutions and will inevitably harm your results.

As you plan for your desired results and achievements, do everything in your power to think in terms of possibilities, not obstacles and problems. Whether you think about problems or not, they will most likely end up across your way. I am by no stretch of imagination suggesting that you not have any contingency plans or exit strategies in case things do not quite work the way you want. However, you must restrict this to a minimum, as your energy and time must be focused on realising your ideal result and giving it all that you have.

MASTER GIFT CLUSTER

Let's attach another piece to your planning process to create impossible speed in your results. You have been given, and you may have developed at least to some extent, a master gift cluster. So what is it?

Your master gift cluster refers to any specific combination of gifts and talents unique to you, that allows you to perform at a superior level and contains a contributing ability to better your life environment. It is very important to understand that your gift cluster is not designed as an instrument of sole self-satisfaction. Your gift cluster is both a gift to you and gift to those around you. Before attempting to define it, let me help you identify what it leads to, as you have most likely already experienced the benefits of functioning with the aid of your gift cluster.

The first thing that you experience when harnessing your gift cluster is the comments of your family or peers saying "You are a natural!"; "You learn so fast; where did you get that from?"; "I can't believe how good you are in these circumstances"; "Come on, stop telling me that this is easy"; "That is so unfair; I wish I could do that"; "How did you get so much done in so little time?" Sound familiar? Your gift cluster gives you superior power to do the things you want to do. By learning to recognise it, develop it, and focus your activities on it, you become capable of boosting your performance without sweating to achieve your results. It is like a natural life result accelerator with no harmful side effects.

Your gift cluster will cause you to become more effective and to have more determination and energy. It will cause you to experience a sense of ease where there was strife, a sense of peace where there was unrest and possibly stress. If you are overstressed in your life or your professional activities, take it that most likely you are not functioning in harmony with your gift cluster. You have heard that the secret of success is being at the right place at the right time. I do not disagree, but this is most likely out of your control, so I suggest that you look into positioning yourself within your gift cluster so that when you are at the right place at the right time, you can capitalise on it.

Your life gift cluster can be defined as the combination of:

- **Your dominant master skill set (what you are very good at)**
- **Your dominant interpersonal temperament (how you interact with others)**
- **Your dominant difference-making passion (what you enjoy doing for others)**
- **Your dominant life theme (the thread of consistency of your life)**

PERSONAL VALUES

Materialism attaches possessions as the condition and realisation of your happiness. At the other end of the spectrum, spiritualism often looks for detachment from possessions as a condition of happiness. Living within your gift cluster is a creative process of emergence where you will find more of your own value for yourself as you understand your contributing power towards other people's happiness and find great reward in financial and emotional basis in all that you do.

Every person has a preference towards certain things that they value more than others. These possible values have infinite facets, as every person is unique, and your own value set is unique. However, they will fall into primary categories of life expression. These categories are Personal values (what I desire for myself), Social values (what I value for those around me), Material and Financial values, and Spiritual values (my perception and expectation of spiritual nature). Important: values are not goals! Goals are actually attached to our values. Example: your goal might be to buy a new house, but your value attached to this goal is "comfort and security". You may desire a new sports car as a goal, but the value might be "being noticed" or "thrill of speed". I personally came to realise that my top values are the very program of all that I do, and being aware of it has provided me with a compass and checklist to ensure that I am building in the right direction.

I cannot act in any direction at all until I find a clear convergence with my number-one value, my relationship with God. Unless it meets this criteria, this filter of decision making, I cannot launch anything. Second, I will never attempt to construct any system or business direction that does not allow for my relationship with my wife and children to flourish, as my family is my number-two value, and so on. When it comes to seeking financial prosperity, you better be sure that finances are high on your value scale or that you clearly understand how money serves your values. Otherwise you most likely will not find the needed momentum of energy and inspiration to accomplish what you want. Conversely, if you give it all on a professional basis and are successful at the price of your personal relationships when "nurturing your children" or "emotional intimacy with your spouse" is your primary value, you will find yourself at the head of a nightmare with your life falling apart. If that is your experience, don't reason it out but restore proper order in your business and life plan so that it meets your values and the values of your spouse. In doing so you will regain control of the situation... After all, is not racing all about the quality of your control? Let's have a look.

RACING CONTROL

CHAPTER 21

Race-car driving and control are synonymous. After all, every component on the car is designed to give control to the race driver. As you can imagine, the complete steering mechanism is designed to execute a three-way control combination of the driver, car, and track. The steering input of the driver has to deliver great accuracy from the steering wheel throughout the whole mechanism to the final recipient, the front wheels of the car, while providing the feedback to the racer so he can adjust adequately. In everyday driving, we associate steering with direction change only. In race driving, steering involves both the execution of a race line and also the dynamic influence on the car in order to control its behaviour as a whole at race speed.

For the 2009 race season of the American Le Mans Series, Acura and Wirth Research of England developed a new concept for their new Acura ARX02-a LMP1 prototype, putting the same size tire at the front of the car as at the back! To the casual observer, this may not be such a big deal, as most cars have four tires of the same size. Well, here is the deal: in racing, the front tires are narrower because the force that it takes to steer them is excessively huge. A narrower race tire at the front of a Le Mans prototype is still three times larger than those on a sedan; now, with the front tires the same size as the back tires, they would be four to five times larger. Everyone loved the idea, as the regulations allowed it, but no one had found a way of compensating for the technical difficulties of steering dynamic forces and the increase in aerodynamic drag, which resulted in airflow disruption at high speed. Wirth Research, however, found a way and did not give up during testing times, although there were some issues with hydraulics – once again, because of the gigantic forces required to turn these front-end tires at race speed. The benefit came in the form of greatly increased front grip as the contact patch of the tires increased, resulting in greater cornering speed. The engineers' aim was to increase overall performance, but it came with a price tag. Compromises had to be made and creative solutions implemented in order to benefit from this. Finally, the success in engineering terms was only validated as the Acura prototype performance proved superior and the racer at the wheel could exercise proper control without exerting himself.

Like Acura's elite team, you have to determine your control factors in order to generate the results that you want. It is not enough to set out in a new direction; you have to ensure not only that you are going where you want to go but that the overall result will be satisfactory to your final objective.

In order to be successful at the steering wheel of life, you have to be aware of all that you can control and influence to maximise your results. You cannot take responsibility for 30 per cent and expect 100 per cent results. You have to move into total ownership responsibility of the problems that need to be solved in order to maximise your influence on the outcome. There is a fine line between controlling constructively and being a controlling individual – the second being negative. A race driver who is controlling will not get the best out of his race car. He must learn to drive the car, which has its own temperament and needs cooperation, not controlling action, to produce a maximised controlled outcome. True maximised control of outcomes is always in leadership and never in force.

Being controlling is often rooted in insecurity and even fear. When you are a confident leader of your life and other people, you do not need to be controlling. A controlling race driver will be tense at the wheel, damaging his lap time and performance.

So become a master of controlled results by, first, understanding that you are meant to be a leader not a controller. Second, take 100 per cent responsibility for all that you can change even though it may hurt, and develop the habit of measuring your actions against your desired outcome and bringing ongoing correction if needed until you achieve your results.

RACING TO THE FINISH LINE

CHAPTER 22

Racing with the finish line in mind is one of the most important qualities, and it can take awhile to develop in younger drivers. Whether you are in the car or watching as a race fan, starts are always a heart-pounding moment as thousands of horsepower are about to be released in a fraction of a second. The tension mounts steadily before the green flag is waved, and this can be rather unbearable and nerve-wracking even for experienced people. Every start is a new start and can be full of surprise and drama.

The American Le Mans is an endurance racing series, which, as in life, is never won on turn one. When you think about all of the racing that will take place and add to this the pit strategies and the tire and driver changes, a race victory is the assembly of a lot of things that have to go right. I still remember the devastated and exhausted look on my friend Terry Borcheller's face, despite his stunning performance at the 2005 Mosport Grand-Prix.

The weekend had been perfect, and the Saleen SR7 GT1 car had been finally outperforming the Factory Corvettes during practice and qualifying. Now Terry and his co-driver, Johnny Mowlem of England, were leading comfortably on race day, steadily pulling away from Corvette and certainly keeping them at a comfortable distance. Then disaster hit, not on the race track but at their last pit stop. Due to a refuelling issue, the race was lost in the last final minutes. It had been perfectly run until that moment, the effort of the team and skills of the drivers were second to none, and yet they lost to something which could have been definitely avoided. I am not trying to stir difficult memories; after all, that's racing, and racing is like that: often unfair even to the well prepared. I simply want to point out that racing for a win and crossing to the finish line requires that every single aspect of a winning combination be carefully monitored, maximised and if necessary, improved upon, over and over, until there is a virtually absolute guarantee that it will work.

When you are racing to the finish line, you are not putting on a short-lived stunt performance. You are committed to the race that you really want to win, and you race it in a way that will make the most out of who you are and what you can achieve. No matter the outcome: win, lose, or draw, you will keep your head up and will be able to say, "I pressed on towards the prize; I did my best to the chequered flag. I gave it all my very best, and I am a winner!"

ROOKIE RACING

CHAPTER 23

Bringing rapid change into your life and your business will require that you make new decisions. And every time you make a decision towards creating new realities to generate new results, you are starting over again as a rookie!

You are the rookie of the new class of success into which you are engaging, regardless of what you have done before. You are pushing the borders of your previous limits of achievement. No matter what kind of previous achievements you may have and regardless of your experience or status in life, if you are going not only for more of what you already have but for new and greater levels, you will somehow start once more as a rookie!

When you look at it from this standpoint, you realize that what a rookie does is not really realistic. Why? Because he or she has not done it before! The first time I raced in a rally in France, I was a rookie: I had been to rally school and had been driving for years, but I had to learn everything about rallying.

How can you forget your first race? I still remember it vividly. It was near the French Alps on a nice country road, a type of racing called hill climbing. As I was waiting for the green light, my eyes were riveted on the road ahead; I was ready to unleash the fury! At the first turn, as my slick tires had not built temperature yet, I nearly scared the life out of myself. I had never driven on slicks before and was not aware of tire temperature effect. I was just expecting this massive grip from those awesome race tires, which, unfortunately, were a few months old, and the compound was too hard for my road conditions. I had been sold the wrong tires by a racing family member who took little precaution to warn me, obviously not a great mentor. No grudge, however, as I learned my lesson very quickly. At the second round, I mounted my set of soft tires, and I was flying! As I responded quickly and adequately to the problem, I managed to finish third in class that day, taking my first podium for my first race!

Had I been realistic based on my past achievements, I would not have started the race in the first place. I did not have the financial means to do testing, and owning all kinds of tire sets was not an option. So when I decided to just do it, I learned that being unrealistic is the only gateway to forming new realities. With experience comes realism again, which will carry you to the top of your game. In this, unrealism and realism are not in opposition but rather are working in cycles. Excess of either is never a good thing, but proper use of both is a powerful combination to accelerate your results.

Unrealistic dreamers are at the forefront of enterprise and inventions. They light up the world, power our machines, invent new technologies, and transform markets because the image they have in their mind might be unrealistic to others, but it is very realistic to them. Through the creative process of thought, they are able to overcome any obstacles in their way to achieving their idea.

Don't worry about being unbalanced at first; balance will catch you soon enough, and mastery never precedes achievement – it results from it. As a matter of fact, as you let your ally named Wisdom work with you and be your guide, you might be surprised to discover that more often than not, the call of wisdom will feel very unrealistic to your "educated" senses! Wisdom knows that you must be an unrealistic rookie before you become a master.

RACING MENTORS

CHAPTER 24

Race drivers can flourish at impossible speed when placed in a mentoring environment. People who think that success in racing is just a question of money and opportunity do not understand racing. The mentoring environment in all the facets of racing plays a big role in today's complex racing world. We do speak about driver development programs more and more, and the same is true about personal development. But personal and professional development is truly accelerated when you learn from mentors and do what they tell you.

A mentor is not a babysitter and is not going to spoon-feed you. However, he will give you key advice and actions to be taken that will further your results. I remember that in my early rallying days, I happened to have a very experienced co-driver. On race day, during a rally stage featured on a fairly narrow and very twisty road of the French countryside, I was pushing my car, passing 150 km/hr, when I entered a long right hander with tall trees hiding its exit line. During the pre-rally reconnaissance, we had written all necessary pace notes that help a rally driver to prepare for the road ahead and avoid treacherous surprises while maximising his speed. As my co-driver was reading the pace notes, which seemed plenty fast to me, he announced, "Floor it and don't let go" and… "It will pass." I clenched my teeth, tensed my wrist on the wheel, and pressed down nervously the accelerator and… it did pass – even without much struggle. The car was willing to do something that I did not think it could handle. At the end of the turn, we were flirting with 170 km/hr on our way to about 200 km/hr towards the bottom of the hill. My willingness to trust my mentor earned us a fifth time on that

105

stage and quite a few compliments on our performance from my peers. The truth is that I could not have done it alone.

If you do what your mentors tell you to do, you will inevitably accelerate your progress well beyond your wildest dreams. The reason is that your performance in any area of your life is limited to your current level of knowledge and application. As you humble yourself and accept the view of a qualified individual who is willing to teach you the things you need to learn, you will catapult forward. It will not be easy or comfortable, but it will be very effective.

So, where are you going to find these mentors? For years I complained that I could not find the right people to hang out with who could help me to succeed. The truth of the matter is that your mentors tend to be outside of your circles of relationship. We always tend to gravitate towards like-minded people who produce like-minded results. This is good for the feeling of comfort of a pat on the back, but not good to move forward. If you only want to entertain a theory about change, keep entertaining the same relationships that you have always had. If you want to actually experience change in your life, be very intent on building new relationships conducive to new results. What do you desire? Financial knowledge: you can register for one of the many free information conferences on investing and seek the company of well-respected people. New parenting skills for your teenagers: how about asking acquaintances and neighbours who you think are doing well with their teenagers to give you a few pointers? New sales results: no point arguing about the product performance; just go out there and ask for the input of other sales reps who do better than you do, and if necessary, have the boldness of asking someone outside of your industry to explain what they do over a cup of coffee. I have done it more than once and have always learned something new and helpful. If you present your request properly, they will give you 20 minutes. I promise you that not many people are doing this, and you will stand out immediately by your stance. You can also attend seminars with great mentors or read their books and take action on their advice. The information available out there is more than anyone can handle, so set your mind to finding it and start growing right now into the person who will achieve the impossible results that you have set out to.

Michael Schumacher, seven-time Formula 1 champion, is known for asking questions wherever he goes to people from whom he thinks he can glean some knowledge. That is a habit of learning from others that has served him well and has certainly never taken away from his amazing ability to dominate his sport. Learning from others is a skill and an attitude. The insecure and self-preserved do not and suffer for it. The wise and confident do it over and again and experience great success as a result.

PART 5
THE RACER'S EDGE

SPECIAL BREED

CHAPTER 25

Racing in a high-speed environment is no walk in the park. The temperature in an ALMS prototype's cockpit can reach temperatures upward of 100°F. It's almost like a sauna on wheels! Don't forget that you are wearing a helmet; add to this a flame-retardant material undergarment made with Nomex, covering your whole head and body, as well as a full Nomex race suit and gloves. With such high temperatures, combined with the need for maximum concentration and the physical demands of racing a car at very high speeds, your mental edge is quickly challenged to the extreme. The ability to perform under those highly demanding conditions will be one of the factors in determining the winner of a race.

When asked to define a true champion, Derek Daly, ex-Formula 1 driver and author of a phenomenal book called *Race to Win: How to Become a Complete Champion Driver*, gives a very insightful view into the makeup of a champion driver.

> **"BOLD, DEFIANT, AND UNFLINCHING. THIS IS A REAL GLIMPSE INTO THE MIND OF A COMMITTED CHAMPION."**

This is not the definition of your average driver. It refers specifically to a committed champion. Daly refers to commitment as the top quality in producing a full-size champion. As an ex-Formula 1 driver, he is quite well positioned to bring this to our attention. Only the committed champions will experience a real results acceleration that will allow them to build momentum of significance leading to superior results. You must keep in mind that only sustainable results produce real winners.

Commitment has often been used as a dissertation subject, or refers to the quality of exceptional people. However, the reality of commitment has tremendous implications. Commitment is one of these words that describes simultaneously the inside and outside of an individual. You cannot be committed without action, and you cannot act your way to commitment without an attitude of total engagement. Total engagement, as opposed to flirtation with desire, is really a true heart matter. You cannot act committed before you are committed inside yourself. The very core of your being, which I refer to as your heart, is the place where commitment finds its home.

Commitment should never be looked at as a form of glorified grudging or grinding of the teeth until the storm passes. It is indeed a whole engagement, a wilful decision to persist until you are in a position to live out the very thing to which you are committed, no matter what the cost. It is worth pointing out that most of the time there is a direct connection between the importance of your goal, the depth of your commitment, and the rewards associated with success. The greater your commitment, the greater the cost, the greater your reward. Any world-class racer knows this. There will be plenty of sacrifices needed if you are to make it to the top and stay there. It is your attitude of perseverance that expresses your inner commitment. There will be challenges ahead to keep on testing you, proving that you are indeed a true champion.

In the description of the committed champion by Derek Daly, we find strong attributes: bold, defiant, unflinching. All of these traits are profoundly true and so important to understand in order to become a full life and business champion. If you are willing to dig deep and attach to your mind the ideas of boldness, defiance, and total determination, you will live at the maximum of your potential.

Always remember that commitment gives hope, hope gives courage, and courage feeds your strength, which will cause you to succeed in all that you do. Live like a true champion, a committed champion!

THE COMPLETE DRIVER

CHAPTER 26

Now let's dive into the specifics of your winning combination. We cannot excel at everything, but we must become excellent regarding the skills needed to accomplish our true desires and the virtues required to support these achievements. Great ALMS drivers like Brazilian Gil de Ferran, Scot Alan McNish, Australian David Brabham, and many others all have a superior set of skills that they have diligently sharpened to achieve their outstanding success. These men and many others have developed their "impossible speed" by using a functional combination of factors that allows them to become and stay successful.

Gil de Ferran did not start racing in Karting until the age of 14 years, and yet he became a multi-time Indy Champion and a Formula 1 technical director, and he recently owned and piloted the Acura Prototype LMP1 #66 in the ALMS. Gil de Ferran is known for his "commitment to results" and "high work ethics" as recalls Jim Hall, who gave him his first opportunity to compete in professional racing. Alan McNish is recognized as one of the brightest and most accomplished drivers on the planet with a career spanning over two decades, from Formula 1 to twice overall winner of the 24 hour of Le Mans with AUDI and countless other championships in endurance racing. David Brabham was already 17 when he first started Karting and yet quickly moved into the ranks of race aces in Formula circles. In 2009, he is over 40 years old and just finished an explosive year with success with the ALMS LMP1 championship title with Acura as well as with the 24 hour of Le Mans as overall winner with Peugeot.

It is now your turn to find your winning combination to achieve superior performance in your personal life and business.

Now let's look at five markers of high performance in life and business:

1. Passion
2. Winning mode
3. Skill set
4. Commitment to ongoing development
5. Willingness to persevere until it is done

1. PASSION

It can be tricky to define passion, as it is systematically employed in so many contexts. Here we refer to a "true burning desire" that has the virtue of honesty, integrity, and contribution. Any desire that is all about yourself without contributing to other people's lives will with time leave you with little more than regrets. You may have succeeded in such circumstances, and you got what you wanted, but it comes with a bitter aftertaste, as you wonder if it was worth it and question the fundamental value of your achievements. The fulfilment of a true desire has a greater dimension than your own self-gratification. It functions beyond the impulse dimension and is easily recognisable as it contains the seeds of growth for yourself and contribution for others. Function in "full-throttle mode"; let your inspiration engine run free, and understand that everything you are and everything you do has a much greater dimension than self-gratifying ambitions. Turn your talents over to greatness by understanding the fullness of your true passion or desire. You then will be able to anchor its fulfilment by understanding your winning mode.

2. WINNING MODE

By now you know that winning in world-class racing, particularly in endurance racing, requires a lot more than going fast. You know that a true world-class achiever depends on a specific winning combination that will take place within his or her winning environment. How many times have you heard, "I was at the right place at the right time"? This has personally left me wondering not only how to get to that point, but also worried that I might miss the boat, so to speak. However, the combination of the right place and the right time happens nearly naturally when you perform in accordance with your winning combination.

A winning combination refers to the convergence of your thoughts, mental state, diligence, and strategic positioning in your critical skills. Every driver has a different winning combination. All drivers want to win, but they have different ways of getting there. Some will be driven to put pressure on other drivers, which is totally acceptable. Some will be on outright blazing speed, some will be on well-timed passes, others in clean driving and staying out of trouble while counting on their team strategy. The point here is that all of them work. Every driver might even use a particular winning combination in one race and another combination in another race; this shows levels of maturity and adaptability.

You have to choose your own winning mode by recognising what works for you and, almost more importantly, what does not work. If you are not a strategist, stop acting like one or even trying to become one. Partner with someone who is, and focus on your strength. If you are organised but lack the flame of enterprise and are weaker in initiatives, partner with someone who has the skills that you lack, and certainly at least ask for help. Acknowledging what we do not have allows us to zero in more easily on what we have and develop better functionality with others.

Once you know what your winning combination is, you will think the right thoughts, be in the right state of mind, act diligently over sustained periods of time, and focus on your core skills. All the while you will remain open to sharing your success with others as you open yourself to their support. You will function at peak performance with less stress and greater flexibility while adding tremendous enjoyment to your endeavours.

3. SKILL SET

Identifying your core skills and the core skills required to achieve your specific goal is both critical and rather simple. Whether you want to lose weight, develop romance in your marriage or relationship, or create a new start-up or new department in your company, the same rules apply. Excellence must be developed in those core skill areas. The key here is development. No one was ever born mature and equipped for business, but we are given the ability to learn what we do not know. The phenomenal amount of knowledge available nowadays through books and interactive media is breathtaking. You can simply make a decision, do some quick research, and start learning your new skill.

In business, it is important to understand that a company that "demands" increase in results and requires change in behaviour without the corresponding "investment" in helping its people can run itself into a serious discrepancy between expectations and results. Properly investing in your people's skills is as crucial as planting seeds. No one would ever expect to harvest a field of corn without having first sowed corn seed. Things always grow after their own kind. Want a different harvest, different results? Look at what is being sowed in principle and applications, and start correcting as necessary.

4. COMMITMENT TO ONGOING DEVELOPMENT

Nothing remains still. Bob Proctor states: "**If your life is not going in one direction, by law, it is going in another direction.**" Do not get trapped into stillness and the comfort zone, as it is rampant with all kinds of non-acceleration elements. Imagine what the mindset of a racer would be if his thought logic went like this: "Since I won that Grand Prix three or four years ago; therefore, I am competitive to win today!" Everyone would laugh at him, including the non-experts in racing. This is presumption and not confidence. However, we can find ourselves caught in this paradigm, enjoying our success at its peak and forgetting the very things that brought us there. This is where the up and down results come from. When I stop applying myself to sharpening my skills through ongoing development, my skills become dull, and this leads to disappointing results.

Developing our skills should be a constant progression. Moving your life into the fast lane means that you must be fully alert and on top of your game; otherwise you risk losing the ability to successfully navigate challenges. This is referred to as the car-racing you. When your race car goes ahead of where you are mentally, performance dips quickly, as you lose your sharpness of input and find yourself reacting to the car instead of directing your vehicle. Fatigue is one of the primary enemies, as it is conducive to this type of reactive racing. In life and business, the fatigue of daily pressure can cause you to feel like you are not in control anymore, as though the vehicle is racing you. If that is the case, you need to regroup and rest for awhile. You certainly cannot develop your skills in such conditions, regardless of how hard you try. Be committed to going where you want to go. Stay alert; sharpen your skills, like a champion who takes full responsibility for his results.

5. WILLINGNESS TO PERSEVERE UNTIL IT IS DONE

Sometimes excelling at impossible speed means having to persevere in times of dynamic waiting. Dynamic waiting? Is there such a thing? Yes, and it is the opposite of passive waiting. In dynamic waiting, you are proactively waiting for things to catch up and allow your success. Persevering means that sometimes you have to acknowledge that since not everything is about you, but also about your partners, your clients, your spouse, or your children, there may be times when your race car must idle for a short time while other areas are taken care of. You have to acknowledge that they may not be ready to experience with you the desired results and that you may have to do some work with them to prepare them; you must also be patient, not grudgingly but constructively. Don't kick the dirt, don't stamp your feet, but instead, enlarge your understanding and sharpen your discernment. Delay can at times be the strongest ally of functional acceleration. For example, if you were to accelerate too early out of a turn, your race car would surely spin out of control and crash. You have to wait for the right moment and apply the throttle properly or suffer the consequences. Everyone who has driven on a snowy road knows what I am talking about. Perseverance keeps you doing the right thing until the conditions are right and the full acceleration can be unleashed.

THE CHAMPIONSHIP MINDSET

CHAPTER 27

Anthony Robbins is well known for this statement: "The true power of change is not found in right answers but in right questions."

If you wonder what it takes to win in a particular area, you must first ask yourself powerful questions such as, "Why do I want really want to do this, or succeed in that arena?" and "What does success look like to me, in this situation or that situation?" If you invest the time to discern the nature of your desired results, you will be better equipped as a true champion who knows that life is not a sprint or even a succession of sprints but a true endurance race.

No matter what area of life you want to succeed in, you are in an endurance race whether you like it or not! Most of your decisions will have to reflect that reality. Many mistakes would be avoided and much heartbreak would be spared if we were to make decisions based on this long-term view instead of on impulsive short-term decisions. How many times have you found yourself wondering: "Why did I do this? I wish I had been thinking about the long-term consequences." The answer is rather simple; you forgot which race you were running, and you may not have even been aware of the race unfolding before you.

When there is a restructuring, new acquisition, streamlining, or downsizing, are we thinking endurance race? Do we operate with long-range vision or with short-sighted, circumstance-pleasing decisions? Only you can answer that question. Some decisions are difficult and some can be outright painful, but you can only make those decisions if you put them in the context of a clear knowledge of the race you are going to win. It is not enough to have strategic meetings to produce real strategy. It is the endurance mindset operating in and powering the thinking of the executives that produces an effective long-term strategy. We must make wise decisions, not feel-good decisions that only address the short-term issues.

Any entity, corporate or individual, that is willing to invest in long-term vision while addressing short-term issues will produce much better results and will certainly engage their human resources in a very different way. We do not live in an easy world; difficult and costly decisions have to be made, but it is only by engaging the long-range mindset of an endurance racer that we can ensure that the decisions will hold up in the light of hindsight.

Winning a world class and prestigious race like the 24hr of Le Mans requires a definite "Endurance Mindset". When the French Manufacturer Peugeot entered its 908HDI-FAP diesel LMP1 prototype, they had one goal—beat dominant Audi. The Peugeot with its impressive closed cockpit Coupe was even nicknamed the "Audi Killer". However when the Peugeot LM prototype was introduced in 2008, despite its stunning speed on qualifying, Audi still dominated the race. There were two primary reasons for that: one, Audi is not interested in qualifying impressions because they focus on the end result of the 24hr, and second, their experience and confidence took them to the top step despite the somewhat superior performance of the Peugeot. However in 2009, it was a different story. Peugeot's determination caused them to keep pushing upward in performance and reliability and Audi was not really capable of holding them back. Peugeot had not only stuck to its 24hr endurance winning capability, but stayed committed to its long range plans to dominate the race despite the economic cost in challenged economic times.

RACE CONDITIONING

CHAPTER 28

In recent years, the sports world has shifted away from the original concept of training to physical conditioning, and even more recently, into sports-specific conditioning. The new conditioning concept tends to recognise that the body, in all of its unfathomable complexity, and the mind, in its endless dimensions, need to be trained simultaneously in both a specific and an interactive way. Instead of isolating drills, the conditioning drills will create a combination of strength, balance, endurance, and coordination, all designed to enhance the overall capabilities of an individual to produce superior results.

Race drivers are progressively exposed to more conditioning, as opposed to the drivers of the past who came to the track to perform and returned home to a less performance-oriented nutrition and lifestyle. Little by little, we are learning that we can influence and learn to create greater opportunity of performance. ALMS prototype drivers are subject to phenomenal physical demands from racing such high-performance machines. The heart-stopping prototypes are rather close in performance to a Formula 1 car, with cornering abilities around 4 G lateral and braking around negative 4 or 5 G. When you are undergoing a 3 G to 4 G turn in your race car, it means that your head, for example, weighs three to four times more than its normal weight. You can imagine the strain on neck muscle with your head weighing over fifty pounds. Obviously, only extensive physical training can allow someone to function with precision and endurance in such circumstances.

Just as race drivers must prepare themselves to handle these extremes, so you, too, must prepare yourself to handle a more intense pursuit of your dreams. Unless you are aiming at becoming a race driver or jet pilot, you may never experience the physical application of G force, but you will experience the emotional and physiological dimensions of a more intense life. This means that you have to become more before you can have more, and that you will become more continually as you live out more of the specific outcomes that you are looking for, whether personally or professionally.

In success conditioning, there is the progressive realisation that yourself comes first and that the rest will follow. This is not a definition of egocentrism but rather the realisation that you have to first venture into the land of change before your results can be where you would like them to be. You want more sales, more money, more health, more peace at home, or better results in your company? Great, be the change you are looking for. Just as the great Mahatma Ghandi said, "Be the change you want to see in the world."

When you engage this type of approach, you are on a continual movement forward even through the most menial things, because you are changing. You become more alert, and what you used to consider unimportant now represents another area of improvement and movement forward. It is fun at times, less fun other times, but always immensely rewarding as you very quickly become hooked on this sense of wholeness and fitting in with life at large.

You will never see a true success-conditioned champion throw his empty lunch bag out the window of his or her car, or absorb hours of junk programming on TV, or be consumed with addictive behaviours including on the computer screen, or crush his employees' spirit, or treat his spouse in a menial way, or ignore the needs of his children, or criticise and gossip for hours on end, or complain endlessly. A success-conditioned person gains incredible inner strength and beauty, which allows him to develop a set of actions that will inexorably lead to the progressive realisation of a worthy ideal – as Earl Nightingale, one of the fathers of personal development, would put it.

It is time to experience impossible speed in your full walk of life; start success conditioning yourself today by immersing yourself in what builds and strengthens. Start reading, start writing, start running, start loving, start doing what you have never done before, and dare to believe that you will succeed with impossible speed and never go backwards in anything.

HAND-EYE COORDINATION

CHAPTER 29

Constant hand-eye coordination is one of the most fundamental skills to be mastered by a race driver. Interestingly enough, any driver uses such a skill but in very basic and limited ways. Indeed, every time you drive your car, you first look where you want to go, then position your steering wheel in such a way that the car goes where you want it to go. However, for a world-class race driver, this skill is developed to a very high level that allows them to control their race vehicle in an extremely precise way and at very high speed.

Mental focus in life and business is strikingly similar to hand-eye coordination in race-driving conditions. In racing, you first perceive through visual input, then process the information mentally, and finally execute it physically. There is a tremendous need to develop a high level of hand-eye coordination to succeed with impossible speed. For this your mind has to be fully engaged within your passion realm as previously developed. You cannot be asleep or even distracted the slightest bit. This aspect creates tremendous satisfaction but also requires more awareness and discipline than average performance. And yes, your focus will create the speed you are looking for. Without it, you may skid off the race line or off the race track too often to produce impossible results. With it, you will accelerate everything you do.

It is easy to lose focus, or not develop focus at all. You can still race with lack of focus, but you are certainly not going to win, and most likely, you may not even finish. Focus is a choice; it is the conscious decision to dedicate your energy in a specific direction over a concentrated period of time. Too often, lack of focus not only leads to lack of results but also damages one's faith and ability to succeed altogether.

BEFRIENDING RISK

CHAPTER 30

Racing at world-class level and with high speed against high-level competition is not possible without acquiring the proper perspective on risk and danger. Depending on the person with whom you speak, you can find all kinds of perspectives and opinions about this. Race drivers typically don't like talking about it; this is not the object of their focus. One thing is certain, however: drivers are not unaware of danger; they just have a unique and supportive relationship with it. This is not avoidance as much as it is knowledge of a very important factor – where your mind goes, so does your life and your results. If you worry about crashing, you most likely will.

One of the first habits to develop in race driving is the need to look where you want to go, no matter what the car is actually doing, in order to maintain control. The concept is simple but very demanding, as we all have a natural tendency to look at what we might hit in order to avoid it. That is a definite problem, as you will end up where your eyes are set whether you like it or not – that is just the nature of the beast. You can argue about this in life, but I promise you that you will never argue about it while race driving; it is an irrefutable fact.

Then the fear factor comes into play, which makes things even worse. When fear comes in, your focus shifts to the object of the fear, and thanks to the previous driving lesson, you now know where you are heading – straight towards the problem, no matter how much you want to avoid it. It is very important to free our mental focus from the negative influence of fear. Focus was given to us to direct us where we want to go, not where we don't. However, you are in charge of focus like you are in charge of the steering wheel. You cannot blame the car for turning right when you steer to the right – and it is the same with focus. Fear will most likely cause us to steer towards the problem. Remember the motto: "Wherever you are looking, that is where you are going."

Often, when disappointing things happen and the pressure mounts, you will find yourself returning to square one. To avoid this and free yourself from the negative influence of the fear factor, let's take things a little further. We can break fear down by understanding that fears are:

1. **Experiential**
2. **Circumstantial**
3. **Attached to self-concepts**
4. **Connected to mental imagination**
5. **The basis of preservation**

1. FEARS ARE EXPERIENTIAL

It is important to realize that fears are experiential in nature. Have you ever wandered in the dark of the night by yourself in some unfamiliar area? As long as you enjoy yourself, all is well. As soon as you start thinking of who could be hiding, ready to jump at you, the hairs on your back might start to rise, and your palms can get very sweaty while your heartbeat increases – all before an outright sense of panic sets in. Yet nothing has happened at all! Fear is an emotion and the expression of a feeling. I want to point out that unless you give it meaning, fear is often even totally unjustified. There is a whole physiological response to fear whether it is justified or not. It causes us to say that fear just "is" because it gets hold of our senses. So what can you do? First, acknowledge that it is a feeling, seek the truth in the matter, be objective, and reengage your mind. Fear cannot take hold of you unless you attach some meaning to it – just like our walk in the dark pointed to it. Fear is never to be looked as an absolute. Since it is not an absolute, it should not be considered an insurmountable obstacle to creating the results you want, and certainly should never stand in the way of your true desires. If you give it this relative meaning as opposed to an absolute meaning, you will free yourself from its grip and start to create change and accelerate your results.

2. FEARS ARE CIRCUMSTANTIAL

Fears may vary, depending on your circumstances. Let's say that you have some fear of speaking to large crowds, and yet you are totally comfortable speaking to your friends or colleagues. The question is: where does your comfort feeling end and your fear experience start? Is there a magic number of people who need to listen to you all at once before your fear of public speaking kicks in? You may also notice that you used to be afraid of speaking to small crowds, but that today you think nothing of it anymore. Where did the fear go? The truth is that fear will evolve with you. But once again, who has been giving it its meaning? You. Since you are the one who is giving the meaning to it, fear has to evolve around you and will therefore be circumstantial; however, it will never be truth, as truth is an unshakable reference, not an evolving reality.

3. OUR FEARS ARE OFTEN FOUNDED ON OUR BELIEF SYSTEM, ALSO CALLED SELF-CONCEPT

A self-concept is a certain viewpoint that you have developed of yourself, sort of an auto-critic. You think you are capable of doing certain things and in a certain way. Without self-concept, you would not really have any sense of identity, any references to operate from. So it is essential that you have a clear understanding of your self-concepts. However, the problem starts when the inner critic (telling you who you are) is rather harsh and non-objective, and stubbornly refuses to make room for transformation when you look at increasing your results. Like an autopilot, it forces you to stick to the flight plan of your personal belief system. Fear will kick in every time you step out the box of your self-concept, called the comfort zone. When you know that the vast majority of self-concepts are set within the first five to seven years of age, you may understand why you feel like things are just the way they are – period.

If you are willing to look deeper into your heart, which is the core of your being, you will find that, regardless of your track record in the past, a flame of hope and faith is waiting to be reinvigorated. It may be small, but it is not out. If you are willing to not listen to fear, guilt, and regrets, but rather choose to let the still small voice in you tell you what you are worth, you will find the courage to overcome the deadliest fears as you go on the journey of redesigning your self-concepts. Redesign self-concept? Yes, you can choose to see yourself differently by creating a new picture of yourself as you would like to become and making this your point of focus. When you do that, although fears will be triggered, they will subside to the new image to which you have shifted your focus. And needless to say, that image has to be about an authentic heart's desire or it will be smashed by the old fear attached to the comfort zone.

4. FEARS ARE MOSTLY ATTACHED TO YOUR IMAGINATION

We entertain fears through our imagination – it is generally put in the form of "What if _____ happens?" For some strange reason, the higher the stakes, the more we seem to be magnetized towards possible negative outcomes. As we engage our acceleration processes and decide to dramatically increase our speed, let's also make use of our fear filters through useful reasoning and acknowledge that we are much bigger than this. It may not be by our own virtue, but by the virtue of the life that sustains us day in and day out. If I were to tell you that I am afraid to run out of oxygen and stop breathing, you would laugh at me. However, there is little difference between being afraid of running out of oxygen, of which none of us control the supply that is abundantly given to us, and being afraid of pursuing our dreams in the name of a possible failure. Use your imagination only to form constructive thoughts for your life and systematically refute the fear of failure by first recognizing that most of the things you feared in the past most likely never happened.

5. FEARS ARE A BASIS OF PRESERVATION

Fear can actually protect you and be your friend. Imagine what would happen if you had no fear of being burned by fire or of falling off a cliff. You would not experience fear, but you would not experience life very long either! No great racer would negate that he or she experiences fear occasionally and anxiety more often. The "constructive fear" of crashing the car indeed allows them to keep within the envelope of performance of the car without destroying it. Such fear is positive because it serves people well and actually contributes to their success. Put out of its context, however, it may turn into a hindrance rather than a help.

Mario Andretti, Formula 1 world champion and American racing legend, put it in a priceless way: *If everything seems under control, you are probably not going fast enough.* How do you know that everything is not under control? You are starting to feel afraid or at least nervous. You will find yourself on edge, which allows you to explore your limits of speed and performance and to keep pushing them farther as your skills increase. So now here is an assessment question for you: "Are you going fast enough?"

PART 6
PART 6: WHEN THINGS GO WRONG

CRASH

CHAPTER 31

As the popular saying goes, racing was born a few seconds after the second automobile had left the production line. Since the earliest days of racing, crashes have always been part of the landscape. In the same way, unexpected and undesired episodes in our lives will cause us to feel like we literally crashed. Whether this will happen at high speed, whether it has to do with life or business, it is not a matter of if but a question of when. The question remains, what do you do when things go wrong?

When a serious crash occurs in racing, it is as though the air comes to a standstill. Eyes are riveted to the scene, and hearts are pounding as a driver could be seriously hurt. Many drivers used to lose their lives in the early years of racing. Some drivers in those days would even confess that they found pleasure in courting danger. Sir Stirling Moss, the famous English champion who was the first one to win the 1955 Miglia in Italy, once said, *"I certainly had an appreciation of the danger, which to me was part of the pleasure of racing. To me now racing is – the dangers are taken away: if it's difficult, they put in a chicane. So really now the danger is minimal – which is good, because people aren't hurt. But for me the fact that I had danger on my shoulder made it much more exciting."*

Danger was a predominant force in racing until F1 race drivers joined forces under Jackie Stewart's leadership in 1973 as president of the GPDA – Grand Prix Drivers Association. In his book *Winning Is Not Enough*, Sir Jackie recounts the many deaths leading to the boycott of the Spa-Francorchamps Grand Prix unless safety measures were taken. He himself escaped the grip of death many times, including in 1966 when he was injured in a high-speed crash with his leg pinned by the steering column in the cockpit with fuel spilling over him. After an unbelievable wait and a long drive in the ambulance, he was flown to England, where he recovered.

Thanks to increased awareness through safety campaigns, safety finally became a priority. The racer became more important than racing itself. Since the loss of one of the most charismatic drivers in history in 1994, Formula 1 phenomenon and world champion Ayrton Senna, there have been very few deaths in modern world class racing. The American Le Mans Series has never lost a driver in ten years of racing. What a beautiful feat!

Racing danger has always been there and will always be there. But our relationship to it has evolved, and the results have become tremendously different. It is my belief that the way we relate and act to "life and business crashes" will make a vast difference in our outcomes.

We can be proactive and plan for the unexpected – that is called contingency planning. This kind of approach will protect the continuum of your resulting acceleration. While it is a fact that being solely positive will not prevent crashes and unforeseen circumstances from unfolding, you will be better prepared to face and rebound from them when they do occur.

However, sometimes even those plans do not seem to match up with reality. What should your response be when things unfold wrong in spite of your best efforts of preparation and contingency? The answer lies in understanding the concept of response maximisation. A maximised response can be many things. Sometimes it will mean actively learning from mistakes and at other times, acquiring new perspectives. It will be finding new levels of motivation to restart. You will be faced with many decisions, and the quality of your decisions will largely dictate what your future will be. When your business start-up does not go the way you wanted, when your marriage sours, when your children do not respond to your best intentions, you will have to make a choice as to how to respond. Regardless of the circumstances, whether you are at fault or a victim of someone else's choices, you must never fall prey to the

RACING STRATEGIES TO CREATE HIGH PERFORMANCE

victim mentality. The victim mindset will launch and plunge you into yet another level of crisis in the form of "why is this happening to me?" Although some useful answers can be occasionally found in response to this question, make sure to not go down the path of seeing yourself as a victim of other people's actions. By refusing to give in to this mindset, you will remove yourself from the frustration caused by success serial killers that express themselves in forms such as: "I did not deserve that"; "if only"; "vengeance will be served"; "how did they dare"; "I will show them what I am made of"; and so on. None of these success pollutants fit the response-maximisation concept, as they do not primarily look to establish you and your pursuit; rather, they try to find answers in the past and justification for how you feel. Maximised response is always established by looking at the future with calm and confidence, based on the values into which you have anchored your heart.

Remember that even the most skilled racers can make mistakes or go off track for reasons totally beyond their control. In June 2008, the #2 Audi R10 TDI was leading the 24 hour of Le Mans by a vast margin. Suddenly with only hours left to race to victory, as the car was entering the fast Indianapolis Corner at the end of the Mulsanne straights with a speed of around 300 km/hr, the rear left wheel of the car broke loose and sent factory driver Dindo Cappello flying out of control into the tire barriers at over 200 km/hr. Thank God, he was not injured in the accident, but despair fell on the AUDI team, and Dindo was totally distraught at the suddenness and finality of the situation. Here is the beautiful side to the story: one year later, they stood on the highest step of the podium in front of 100,000 cheering fans! As professional racers and a racing team, Audi has developed the ability to leave the past behind and rebound without any damage to their assurance and self-confidence. Their winning identity is so strong; they have become virtually unshakable, no matter what racing throws at them.

Anyone with the desire to maximise his or her life must master the art of refocusing rapidly and redirecting all efforts to win again. Once the available answers in the form of "why" are covered, successfully or not, quickly move on and refocus on the next race. Wilfully remove from your mind and heart any "pollution" associated with the crash in order to reengage fully as an undeterred champion and move on to the next achievement point. No matter what happens, you must never be a victim, but a victor in all your circumstances.

Sometimes it may require definite efforts, particularly when you have to forgive those who hurt you. But the pain of forgiveness lasts only the time we wait to forgive. Past the point of forgiveness, there is freedom, movement, and flourishing life again. Then you can reaccelerate your life and your results back to racing speed.

RACING AFTER THE CRASH

CHAPTER 32

*"YOU DON'T JUST DEAL WITH ADVERSITY.
YOU USE IT TO PROPEL YOU FORWARD."*

—Erik Weihenmayer (1968–)
First blind person to summit Mt. Everest

What happens when you crash more than once? How about experiencing extended periods of seemingly unceasing difficulties? I once learned from a great mentor of mine, Jack Zufelt, that there is a greater dimension to decision, which he calls re-deciding. Jack is a renowned speaker and trainer out of Denver, Colorado. He had to personally master this key ingredient of success in order to transform the low self-esteem, failure-bound white boy of a Navajo reserve to become a highly successful businessman in his thirties, finally influencing the lives of thousands in America and overseas! I highly recommend the "DNA of Success" from Jack Zufelt, a must read for anyone who is serious about understanding how real motivation works. Jack even went on to be recipient of the medal of merit from the president of the United States for his contribution to the American people. What happened? An incredible building process, a phenomenal acceleration produced by the ongoing power of true desire and re-decision. Interestingly enough, re-deciding is not a strategy but a particular attitude.

A strategy is something that you execute for a specific outcome for a specific time frame. However "re-deciding" goes beyond that – it is an attitude that stems from a certain mindset and an attitude of faith. I am not referring to religious faith here, although that is the most powerful form; I am speaking about an "attitude of faith" and "expectancy". We have been told, rightfully so, that if we can believe, we achieve. How do you believe? Answer: you truly believe unconditionally and in your heart of hearts, because of your heart's desire and purpose rather than because of your logic or information-processing centres.

In the year 2000, Gil deFerran won his first CART (Championship Auto Racing Team/Champ Car) title after a five-year-long and intense title chase. When you know all that is involved for a racing athlete, that is a lot of time. During that time, you must maintain your champion mindset and confidence. For Gil deFerran it meant: 1995 (rookie of the year) and 1996 saw him grab one win per season. In 1997 he was winless, in 1998 he was winless; 1999 was the first time he had a win since mid-1996. Gil deFerran had to re-decide with every race that he was worthy of victory and relentlessly pursue his aim while convincing others to keep investing in him year after year. Pressure? You better believe it! At the top of his game, Gil joined Penske Racing and was crowned CART champion in 2000 as well as 2001. In 2003, he won the Indy 500. The time of harvest had arrived, and Gil was there to collect the results because he had never backed down during years of trial.

With every re-decision, your strength increases and your resolve solidifies into something virtually indestructible called trust. When you build trust within the meaning of your purpose, it will be extremely hard to get you off course. Let's face it, building strength hurts. Anyone who has ever any done significant physical exercise knows that. In the same way, you might be faced with the decision of having to re-decide despite your current circumstances. At times it really hurts, and you might be thinking that giving up would be an appropriate thing to do, as you may feel too exhausted to keep on racing towards your outcome.

Although giving up is tempting, as it seems to promise the end of suffering, in reality it is no solution at all and even quite the contrary. Lance Armstrong, who has an extraordinary ability to relate to pain, once said, *"Pain is temporary. Quitting lasts forever."* Do not yield to that temptation; awaken the racer in you and go back to racing, as your heart and mind are renewed because of your decision to re-trust and keep on keeping on. Your purpose has to be real, very real, to keep on trusting, to keep on re-deciding. A half-baked motivation, a doubtful purpose, will soon burst into flame as the heat of difficulties intensifies. A true purpose, which is attached to your true passion, survives the heat of trials and comes out to the end with much greater strength, beauty, and power than when you first engaged the process.

Robbie Brozin, CEO of Nando's restaurant, puts it right: "There is a very, very, very fine line between success and failure. It's about being constantly hammered and coming back from the hard times and the low moments." Gil deFerran won his championship title after several years of trials, but who he had accepted to become during that time was essential to the champion whom we so much admire today.

So what are you going to decide and re-decide today? Are you going to go back to this corporate deal that has been so elusive, to this sales goal that meant so much to you, to your spouse and build the marriage of your dreams, to your children and finally breakthrough in your relationship? Are you going back to your health and fitness goal to re-decide that you will not stop until you look like that picture you pinned on your wall? How many times will you have to re-decide? As many times as it takes, because ultimately you are going to win!

CAUGHT IN TRAFFIC

CHAPTER 33

In the unique structure of the American Le Mans Series, with four classes running simultaneously, there is a lot of traffic to deal with. This creates a lot of passing, particularly for the much-faster LM prototypes that lap the slower cars several times during the race. The Grand Tourism (GT) cars have to keep constant monitoring of the rear-view mirror and side windows because oncoming faster cars are racing ahead against each other. Knowing that the races can last from 2.5 to 24 hours in a row, imagine how much traffic must be skilfully dealt with in order to finish successfully. Although in endurance racing, the racing is divided between a team of drivers who have maximum drive time to observe, you can find yourself at the wheel for several hours in a row. Not exactly easy business with such a high-intensity environment!

Inevitably, some leading cars themselves will get caught in traffic, even for a brief moment. They may be held up because of some tight track turns, such as hairpins, or simply because there is too much racing traffic. How frustrating it is when you are driving on the edge, trying to save thousandths of seconds here and there, and you are slowed down by another car for several tenths of a second – or even worse, for several seconds. Knowing that your opponent is behind you, closing in at great speed, while you cannot pass is unnerving. Really, there is no way you can get bored in an ALMS race, as it never stops. It is great for the drivers and great for the fans.

The major issue is in delays that are out of your control. As much as you can be at the right place at the right time, you can also be at the wrong place at the wrong time. Too often, when we encounter extended delays, we can arrive to a critical point at which we have to decide if we are to pursue and persevere or consider other options. This is one of the most difficult things to discern, particularly in a fast-paced world in which we expect results yesterday.

Should you keep waiting and pressing forward, even if multiple signs seem to tell you that it is too late? Tough question... Let's use some assessment tools to help you to evaluate the situation when you are stuck in traffic.

1. **Stuck or re-directed**
2. **Qualify your delay**
3. **Look at possible patterns of delay**
4. **Maintain your speed for reacceleration**

1. STUCK OR BEING RE-DIRECTED

Whether on a personal or business level, experiencing significant delays can be very frustrating and at times lead to outright discouragement. However, we must not arrive prematurely at the conclusion that delays are equivalent to denials. Never make the mistake of arriving at the conclusion that you are being denied a specific outcome without having strongly considered all alternatives. Often when we think it is the end of the road, we find the solution that we have been looking for just around the corner. And more often than not, the solution will be found as we consider the possibility of a course correction or even of a direction change. So how do you tell the difference between a delay and an outright change of direction?

Regardless of the personal or business nature of the delay, we can look at this: in essence, delay is temporary and denial is final. The question then becomes, is there room to operate? Are there conditions that I can influence? Are there items that have been left out and that I need to integrate? Can I leverage this obstacle to turn it to my advantage? Do I keep some measure of control, or is it totally out of my hands? If this leads you to conclude that you do have some measure of influence, then you are most likely facing a delay, and you should not be discouraged. If you arrive at the conclusion that you have done everything there is to do, that nothing else is possible no matter what your resolution, humility, courage, and persistence, then you may have to change direction, at least for now. And if nothing constructive ever manifests with time, you can say with assurance that it was denial – but as you can see, it is not wise to jump to conclusions too fast, as you run the risk of giving up just before the finish line. If denial seems to be confirmed as the definite outcome of the situation, then you can start moving on. Once again, be it in a personal relationship or a business situation, I believe that it is easy to arrive at this terminal conclusion way too soon, well before delay has been understood properly, before all options have been thoroughly explored. So arm yourself with the analysis deployed for you in this chapter, and make sure to stay objective and determined to find the truth of the matter.

2. QUALIFY YOUR DELAY

When faced with delay menacing your desired outcome, remember to qualify the situation! Think about this: we tend to quantify our delay situation as we measure what it is doing against us. We think about how much it costs us financially, in lost opportunity, in lost time, and other quantified measurements. That is fine, but do not forget to qualify delay. Why is this important? Judge for yourself: when you qualify delay, you question its nature. You somehow detach yourself from it, and this allows you to look at it in an objective way. The finger-pointing stops, accusations drop, and you become able to better evaluate what will help you to handle that particular situation. When a delay occurs, ask yourself: "What is the nature of this delay? Is it circumstantial? Is it possibly helpful or detrimental? Is it strictly a practical issue or are there human elements to consider with more of an emotional dimension?" When you question something, not limiting yourself to what it is doing against you, you get back in the driver's seat, you regain a sense of control, and you prevent the situation from controlling you. This is subtle, but it makes for a significant difference as you look for high performance.

3. LOOK AT POSSIBLE PATTERNS OF DELAY

When you tend to experience delays with common threads, it is both very annoying and very exciting. Here is what I mean: every time a new pattern emerges and you understand that there is a recurring phenomenon, you are closing in on the possibility of finding the root cause of the problem. You now have a better shot at truly solving it for the long term. For example, if you are in sales, you might be good at bringing people to the table but poor at closing. It is possible that you will experience the same thing in personal relationships with the opposite sex as you spontaneously initiate a new contact, but when it comes to asking for the date, well, you see what I mean. There you have a pattern that causes you to experience delay in your sales, in your finances, and in your personal life. Tackle the issue by closely examining what might have led you in a certain way of thinking and relating to this. How do you do this?

- **A.** Examine previous situations that contained similar conditions and start to pinpoint these areas where you get stuck over and over (difficulty to close deals, relationships breaking up, debts, unemployment, lack of promotion, business failure, etc.).
- **B.** As you honestly look at these recurring situations, you will probably realise that you have a certain emotional positioning with the issue, a certain way of thinking about it that causes the results again and again.
- **C.** Investigate previous events. Can it be that there is a habit you have acquired after a failure episode? Is there something as far back as your childhood through which you have come to believe that you are just not good enough? Have your parents or anyone in authority in your life spoken condemning words telling you that you were "too dumb" to succeed or "not worthy" of building a lasting relationship?
- **D.** Make a clear decision to think and proceed differently – otherwise you will reap the same problems again. Set your mind on the outcome you are looking for, not what might happen

again, and focus your complete attention and actions on the results that you want. If you don't feel that you are objective enough, I encourage you to hire a coach to guide you through it. But once again, refuse to believe that you are a victim. You are never a victim of the same things repeatedly without one form of consent or another – expressed or silent. Find out for yourself or ask for help, but do not ignore it, as the result will not otherwise be better but most likely worse.

4. MAINTAIN YOUR SPEED FOR REACCELERATION

Acceleration requires a lot of energy, even more than top speed. This can be observed in racing as much as in personal and professional life. Starting and building speed is what requires the most energy in everything. If you doubt this, remember that 90 per cent of business failures occur in the first three to five years. This is why you must do everything to protect your momentum and not come to a standstill while you wait for your desired outcome to materialise. I know what your objection will be: are you telling me to keep going when I am stuck? Isn't that a little contradictory? Well, yes and no. Although your performance is diminished in traffic, you never see a race car stop to create a passing gap. On the contrary, as the traffic approaches, the driver prepares for the next opening by protecting racing lines and racing speed for the best reacceleration possible. You have to project your thinking ahead in order to make the most of the situation and position yourself for passing and reacceleration.

The last thing you want to do when things do not go your way is throw your hands in the air, fuss and fume until it gets better – because on such basis it will not. You are a life racer, remember? You are built for high performance; don't waste it! What would you think of a racer who hit the brakes and screeched the race car to a halt, just because he encountered undesirable traffic in his way that may jeopardise his victory? You would not be impressed, for sure. If things slow down, do not slam your brakes; keep your thinking and action momentum going.

Once again, delays are temporary in nature. Make sure to be perfectly positioned so that when opportunities finally arrive, you can move forward freely again – please be there and at reacceleration speed, or run the risk of being left behind.

Like an ALMS prototype racer, become a master of traffic and learn to make opportunities when others only see problems. Your results will not be short of stunning if you will learn the secret of reaccelerating with impossible speed. Do not forget that many races have been won because of a good restart after a "caution period"; don't miss it! Be ready to reaccelerate!

NOT QUITE YET

CHAPTER 34

Over the last few pages, we have been looking at elements of opposition – things that may stand in your way. However, if you pass the test, you will soon be released to full motion forward again. Everything works in season, and impossible speed thinking will also cause you to accelerate in season. You must learn to work with your environment, not against it. Society, business, and family form that environment, and it is imperative to become skilled at maximising the effect of the constraints coming from it by learning all that you can while you can. I remind you again of blind mountain climber Erik Weiheinmayer's approach: "Don't deal with obstacles!" but rather learn to use them to propel you forward.

Principles of success, including the germination-period principle, are not designed to frustrate you, but to empower you to become more suited to sustaining positive acceleration and results. The germination period refers to the time needed between the time you plant and reap. For a farmer, this is a steady, seasonal effect. For an idea or a desire? That time period could be much longer. For a child, we all know that about nine months have to elapse after conception before a baby is born. For a life project, the start of a new business and its profitability, there will also be a germination period that provides the time for adjustment and acceleration – but also for success or failure if that time is not handled properly.

For multiple reasons, we have been persuaded that through the use of a certain magical power or that miracle formula, you can change everything overnight. You will change the duration of the night, but you will not eliminate it. There will be times of drawback, times of testing, times of preparation, times of sheer nothingness. Will you recognise them and know what to do with them, or will you be kicking and screaming?

Things that oppose you are never there to destroy you and your dreams, but to cause you to think in ways previously not considered so that you can give more power to your acceleration. How do you plan on accelerating without power anyway?

Let's assume that a couple is expecting a child. They are both overcome with joy and celebrate the prospect of having a precious baby. The next day the future mother notices that she is putting on a lot of weight, and within a week she wakes up to contractions. The unassuming husband is alerted by his wife's cries and drives her frantically to the hospital where a little one is born in five minutes. There is definitely something wrong with that picture! Whether you choose to view it from the perspective of the mother or the father – think of the raw panic that you would experience. You are not prepared; you have not had time to even think about this little baby! Too early too fast! You are not conditioned in any way for this new life entering your family and altering your destiny forever. It is precisely all that you wanted, but not the way it was supposed to happen. Is it not fascinating that life starts so small, so vulnerable, so weak, and so slowly?

In race driving, what do you think would happen if, without years of training and preparation, you were allowed to sit at the wheel of a 700 hp, 225 mph prototype capable of cornering with four Gs of lateral force and released in a field of other competing lightning-fast vehicles? First, you would scare the life out of yourself, and you would most certainly head for the fences, not the finish line! I do not mean to insult your driving talent but rather am attempting to address the issue of process and progression that function with time. The better way for my son Joshua and me is to develop our racing skills and experience progressively, to go from success to success; very high speed will come at a later stage, when it can be handled, however soon that is!

The pursuit of our worthwhile objectives is not different – there is a suitable gestation period working in your favour. Sometimes things start accelerating from the get-go; sometimes there will be more elapsed time. When everything seems slow, remember that acceleration happens on time if you have let the process prepare you. Find encouragement where you would initially tend to experience discouragement. See yourself as being prepared for impossible acceleration. How do you use time in your favour? Max Steingart, successful millionaire businessman, once said, "Whatever comes your way, give it meaning and transform it into something of value. Your personal growth is the process of responding positively to change. A precious stone cannot be polished without friction, nor humanity perfected without trials."

So next time you encounter oppositions, delays, mediocre results, and other irritating things, remember to not react like a novice but to respond like a champion. Live life like a professional racer, not like an inexperienced teenager at the wheel of a Ferrari – you now know that high performance is not all about raw speed. Learn precious lessons, and increase your power and competencies. Become a total winner!

PART 7
RACE FUEL

YOUR MOST IMPORTANT INVESTMENT

CHAPTER 35

Assume that all you have and all you will ever be given is $100, and from there it is all up to you. If there were only one investment that you could ever make with your $100, what would it be? Tough question, isn't it?

Forget asset allocation, as you can make only one decision. So what will it be?

When we find ourselves restricted in our options, when we are left with basic or with fundamental choice, then our decisions proceed from a different train of thought, a different set of perspectives. If I ask you to choose between wealth and health, what are you going to say? To arrive at an answer, you will have to ask the simple yet powerful questions: "What is most important?" "What comes first?" "What do I have to focus on now?" "What is the highest priority?" In doing so, you start directing your thinking towards the most essential and the most valuable. You start thinking in a less cluttered way, and you clean out the excess fluff. As you progress, you may end up with a rather different answer than you would have otherwise considered.

When it comes to your $100, you now consider your options and you may be tempted to dig a hole and hide your $100 in it so that you don't lose the money. Not only will that be of no use to you, but your dollars will lose value every day due to the damaging effect of inflation: not good. You also know that if you use the advice that used to serve people well a few years ago, that focused on putting your money in the stock market or in mutual funds, you could join the ranks of those who have experienced what they thought was impossible – lose it all. Pension funds, banks, insurance companies have hit the dust. Accident? No, I don't think so. More like money murder! Now let's try buy and hold? We have come to realize that, although we understand the inarguable logic of it, there is an increasing chance of having nothing to hold on to after awhile in the ever-changing landscape of mergers, acquisitions, restructures, and liquidations. Possible indeed, but is there something better?

What is the best answer possible; what is the best investment? *You are!*

"Wait a minute!" you say. I thought we were talking "financial investment"! Yes, we are. You are not an exchange-traded stock nor are you a mutual fund, and yet you are your most expensive and valuable asset ever. One renowned expert and teacher in wealth development, Dr. Rolf DeRoos, once said: "The most expensive piece of real estate you will ever own is between your ears!" Coming from a real estate millionaire, this is rather revealing.

How do you invest in yourself? The foundational premise is to invest in yourself in a way that will radically alter your thinking forever and for the better. Although I encourage you to read more books like this one or to invest in CDs or seminars, you don't have to start there. The good news is that you don't even need any money to start investing in yourself. All you have to do, for starters, is switch your thinking and start using proper thoughts that lead you on to produce greater results. Almost instantly, you will start altering your results. Then as you are using money to invest in yourself, you will accelerate the process by adding to your own competencies the strength of others; then it starts to really take off. Let me tell you a story that illustrates the point.

There once was a young boy whose family was rather poor. They lived in an old house in a gravel pit. One day the father found an old moped in a lake nearby. Since he was poor, he could have fixed it and sold it, but he made another choice. He extracted the engine, fixed it, and attached it to the young boy's pedal kart. Since there were no brakes, the father even decided to attach the kart to a rope so that his son would not crash around the house.

A few years later, the young lad had developed a real appetite for racing machines and particularly race karts. His family could not afford them, so they borrowed some equipment and used discarded tires from competitors.

One day a local businessman watched the young boy on the race track and was impressed by his driving. The boy's father told the businessman that soon they would have to stop as they could not afford any Karting expenses. The businessman was touched and compelled to take the lad under his care and help develop his racing talent.

As the young boy came back from school one day, little did he know that the businessman was about to make another investment in him in the form of a correction that would break the boy's heart. But this man was wise and knew that this boy had to learn that lesson if he was to succeed in life. The young boy was told that since he had never heeded the request to maintain his equipment, Karting was over – the kart was sold! The young boy's eyes filled with tears, and despair showed on his repentant face. The young boy promised that never again would he fall short in maintaining his equipment and that he needed a second chance.

The second chance was given as the businessman bought a new kart for him – his first new kart! The young boy would never depart from his promise as he grew to become the most successful racer in the history of Formula 1. His name? Michael Schumacher, seven-time Formula 1 champion! Not only did he set a winning record in grand prix, but he set a new standard for racers in sports conditioning and unsurpassed attention to details, even minutia in preparing the cars for peak performance!

You don't need first money to create success; you need life assets. Although money will be necessary to materialise many things, that is never where it starts. It starts with you, so first invest in yourself.

I was faced with this dilemma a few years ago. I was beginning a new career after a prolonged downturn in the aviation market. I wanted to create massive acceleration in my results, so I decided to hire a coach who had knowledge of business processes as well as human-performance development. He was and still is a great coach, but he was significantly expensive compared to the state of my finances at the time. It would take several thousand dollars to create a winning model with him that would allow me to reach my goals. Was it going to work? I needed money as a responsible parent. Was it smart of me to let go of that money, or should I invest it in my retirement plan? I decided to invest in myself first and engaged in the process, and I never regretted it, as I doubled my income that year. The point here is that unless you invest in yourself first, you will miss out on making the right decisions over and again and will delay your acceleration.

Companies are not any different than individuals. Recently we have been in times of economic contraction. To cope with the difficulty, companies tend to cut human resource programs. There is some undeniable logic to that, but there are also two sides to that story. One way to look at it is that much money will be saved; great! On the other side of the coin, money stops flowing where it can produce value and create profit; for that, it must not be spent but invested. In times of recession, winning companies will identify accurately what spending is and will reduce it. They will also simultaneously identify what has a potential for returns and protect it. You have heard the expression, "Never kill the golden goose!" The golden goose who lays golden eggs should never be eaten and must continue to be fed. Otherwise there will be ruin! Feed the goose; fatten it even, as it will lay more eggs. Who is the goose – your people! It is the flow of money invested in people that produces growth, evolution, inventions, solutions, and resolutions. It should never be stopped! If it is, the most valuable asset of the company – its human resources – starts to lose its edge, and soon the overall performance of the company will suffer, resulting in more losses, more cutbacks. At that point, the downward cycle is well on its way.

Unquestionably, it will take visionary courage, valuable programs, and a profound understanding of the value to be cultivated in people in order to go against the popular stream of cost cutting and budget streamlining. Those people and companies who have this kind of forward thinking will carve for themselves a way of success even in recession and will be the first ones bouncing off in more favourable economic times.

Invest in people first and always. Everything else comes after that. Every stunning business success story, from Richard Branson's Virgin Group to Herb Kelleher's Southwest Airlines and all others in between, have always had a priority on investing in people right from the start not after the battle. Warren Buffet once said, "The dumbest reason to buy a stock is because it goes up." Why? Because a stock price is history; it is the result of something that has already happened. Likewise, don't wait for things to get better to invest in your people, as you run the risk of being left behind.

The forward-thinking companies will be at the forefront of complete recovery in difficult economic times. Why? The reason is simple: while others were spending their energy building barns to store grain for the winter, these companies have been sharpening their ploughs for the spring.

RACING BUDGET

CHAPTER 36

Money is like the fuel driving your vehicle. Even though it is not directly the star of the show, without it you will be stopped on your journey. Many people treat money as though it were the ultimate trophy, but this is wrong. Money is a medium of exchange that must have a specific purpose. As you think about the budget that powers your own life, examine what beliefs you have about money. Do you assume that you will make the same type of living that your parents did? Do you think that there is no possible way that you can enjoy an annual income of one million dollars or more? The truth is that there is no immediate limit to the amount of money that you can generate – and that is true in both directions. You can make untold millions, or you can be a pauper; it's mainly a matter of choice. There are many examples that prove that this choice doesn't happen because of the socio-economic class into which you were born. It does not depend on how much education you have and does not stem from luck. It begins with your own concepts about money. T. Harv Ecker in his book, *The Millionaire Mind*, speaks about our money blueprint upon which we build our finances. He associates this money blueprint with the thermostat effect, which dictates how much money we get and keep just like a thermostat would regulate the temperature in our house. I don't know about you, but I am going to make sure that my thermostat is set where I want it to be! We don't expect our room temperature to be at 20°C when it is set at 10°C on the thermostat. The same goes with finances; we must first raise the thermostat and then enjoy the change in temperature.

Do you have the ability, and hopefully the courage, to imagine a new and better life for yourself? That which you can imagine and believe until it is materialised through appropriate action, you can create. This is because once you believe that there is more out there for you, you will start acting in a way that will cause the obstacles to start melting away. But if you are convinced that you are destined to scratch out the barest living and refuse to hope for more, then it will never come into existence. You choose your outcome by first sitting and imagining in great detail the outcome you desire and then striving boldly towards that result.

A very wise man once said that money isn't good or evil; it only allows us to become more of what we already are, amplifying the deepest secrets in men's hearts. Had you ever thought of money as a revealer of human hearts and a magnifier of belief systems? This is definitely an uncommon view, which can in itself generate uncommon results.

Examine yourself and discern what is causing you to not have the money you desire. Based on my personal experience and the experience of countless others, there is no easy and quick answer, but it is certainly very worthy of effort. You can really transform your future if you are willing to do whatever is necessary to transform your beliefs about money.

PARTNERSHIPS

CHAPTER 37

Sports-car racing is full of examples of successful partnerships. It is quite common to find a prototype chassis, say from Lola or Zytek, powered by a Mazda, Judd, or AER engine. Only major car manufactures like Audi, Peugeot, Porsche, and Acura have had the critical size and means to develop prototypes in both chassis and engine capacity. Apart from that, there is also a remarkable and ongoing partnership between the American Le Mans Series, the race teams, the sponsors, the advertisers, and the corporate partners. It is beyond a shadow of a doubt that any significant race series is a very complex endeavour and is certainly not a "do-it-all-myself" operation! Under the leadership of Scott Atherton, who is also the CEO of the Panoz Motorsport Group, the ALMS has grown into an extremely successful world-class series. Recently Scott Atherton and his team have formed a new powerful and trend-setting partnership.

World-renowned SAE International, global mobility standard association and its Global Automotive Business director, David L. Amati, reported in their March 2008 update: *EPA, DOE, and SAE partnerships ALMS announced the creation of the Green Racing Challenge. This new competition will encourage manufacturers to introduce and develop their "green" technologies and will be an incremental element of the series' signature event – the 1000-mi (1609-km) Petit Le Mans... partnering with the American Le Mans Series will further allow SAE International to challenge the future of global mobility engineering and the way we all use energy.*

Now this is a real partnership and entails racing with a purpose beyond racing itself. This kind of distinction sets the American Le Mans Series apart and explains its continual growth even as other series are experiencing some contractions in their business.

Steven K. Scott is a highly successful entrepreneur and teacher at heart. In his book *The Richest Man Who Ever Lived*, he describes how he grew a multimillion-dollar annual income after failing nine corporate jobs. In his tenth attempt at anything worthwhile, he used the principles that he teaches in his book and the power of partnerships effectively. The important part here is "knowledge and counsel outside of yourself".

Functional partnerships are even greater, as they aim at compounding the value of each individual or corporation involved in the partnership. This is my favourite type of partnership, as it leads all parties involved to create more success and wealth than they ever could have done on their own. That is why corporations can generate wealth well beyond individual capabilities.

In a marriage, husband and wife are partners. Their marriage partnership is therefore a place of contribution in which they generate greater life results in the form of happiness and fulfilment for each other – all divorce statistics to the contrary. Is it possible, however, that a lack of understanding of the dynamics of partnership in a marriage relationship is at the root of this failure rate of pandemic proportion? This is not a marriage counselling book, but if you look at your relationship with a champion mindset, you will come to realise that your ability to contribute as a partner to your marriage, and vice versa, is essential for the growth and development of that partnership. If left uncared for and not contributed to, soon this partnership will start to go sour.

There is a key question to ask that can change everything in your experience of partnerships. Am I willing to give to the partnership ahead of my own interests? If you can answer yes to that and your partner does the same, then what you will get out of it will be far beyond what you invest into it. Like a race team with a clear objective – racing to win – it does not matter who is right as much as making sure that the team wins. Each team member watches out for each other's interests, knowing that everyone is critically important for the overall team performance. This may sound like utopia at first glance, but you will astound yourself at your business and life experience when you become willing to serve other people's interests.

Andrew Carnegie, who was a legendary figure and the richest man of his time, the epitome of American success, a wealthy industrialist as well as philanthropist, puts it this way: ***"No man will make a great leader who wants to do it all himself, or to get all the credit for doing it."*** As you take one step back and open your circle of influence to others, when you acknowledge that you need the cooperation of equally valuable partners, you have taken the first step towards building an amazing partnership.

You often hear about being careful with whom you associate yourself in business, and I cannot agree enough. Your choice of partners, whether in life or business, will to a large extent command your personal destiny and that of your business. It is critical that you seek and attract the right partners to accelerate the realisation of your results. Your choice of partners can either accelerate your failure or your success – make sure to get the right side of the coin.

So who are these partners? They may be experts, coaches, key employees, executives, certified counsellors, authors, or trainers. The range is immense as you follow the core principle of "sound counsel", which you seek in the form of advice or participation. Whether you are looking for partnership in professional or personal arenas, you want to go through this eight-point track-marker list to assist in your decision.

Track Marker #1: Make it clear that partnership is foundational to your approach.

Track Marker #2: Know what you desire from your partners.

Track Marker #3: Have a crystal-clear common vision of what you are building together.

Track Marker #4: Let your partner come "into" your vision and bring in his own creativity.

Track Marker #5: Do not persuade your partners; inspire them.

Track Marker #6: Be vulnerable and available.

Track Marker #7: Seek your partners' interests.

Track Marker #8: Honour your partners in times of success and support them in times of difficulty.

Track Marker #1: Make it clear that partnership is foundational to your approach.

You must make clear from the get-go that you are seeking partnership and are committed to developing that partnership over an extended period of time. Partnership is not a flirtation; rather, it functions best when all parties seek extended success over long periods of time.

Track Marker #2: Know what you desire from your partners.

You cannot be given what you have not asked for. Your partners feel a lot more useful when they have a clear understanding of what you expect from them.

Track Marker #3: Have a crystal-clear common vision of what you are building together.

Time to build: what does it look like? Have you established common visions and goals? The prospect of common success is attractive, but the road to success is paved with landmines. Make sure that reality does not steal the romance of partnership. The remedy? Know what you are committed to delivering, and know your partner's expectation concerning you.

Track Marker #4: Let your partner come "into" your vision and bring in his own creativity.

A partner is not an assistant, but an equal-value contributor to the desired results. Do not fear your partner's input, even if it is different from your own. Learn to trust your partners as much as you trust yourself. Welcome their creativity, and let them leave their mark on the task. No one takes pride in someone else's achievement, but in their own. Let success flow freely; do not over control!

Track Marker #5: Do not persuade your partners; inspire them!

Partnership is not about who is right but "what" is right. Persuading partners is a fundamental mistake. If you sell your partners on your ideas, they will only think like you. You will miss out on the partnership leverage. If you inspire your partners, they will be empowered to come join you in the game and cause everyone to succeed at much higher levels.

Track Marker #6: Be vulnerable and available.

Successful partnership is not the battle of the Titans! Don't be afraid to ask for help. Should you fall short of expectations, do not hide but be open and find a solution together. Sooner or later, it will be your turn to come to the rescue of your partners.

Track Marker #7: Seek your partner's interest.

You may have heard what many people refer to as the Golden Rule: "Do to others what you would like them do to you." If you can grasp the significance of this perspective, you will put it to work right away. By seeking your partner's interest, you are not negating your own. You are valuing first the "dynamic" of your alliance, and you will benefit from your common success.

Track Marker #8: Honour your partners.

So who's going to get credit when success occurs? Is it going to be all about you? Would that be fair? Personal glory is not that important in a true partnership. Your reward is that you have succeeded where many people failed – in working for a common cause in which the common benefits are more important than one's achievements and personal glory.

How do you partner with anyone when you are in a standalone job like sales? My answer to that, after many years of successful selling in both corporate and direct sales, is that salespeople are way too concerned with their individual performance to the detriment of being part of a successful story. Conversely, some organisations do not make the sales force a strategic point of investment for growth and success. It is not enough to expect success out of salespeople to get sales success; you have to create a culture of success that will become the environment in which people grow. Awards and incentives are great but will not replace ongoing culture and leadership development. Legendary people like Mary Kay Ash demonstrated this truth with staggering results; she created an empire of independent salespeople in over 37 countries. She is famous for many things and in particular, for two of her most notable principles. Her strongest slogan was "First God, family second, career third" (not exactly your average company statement), and "Everyone has an invisible sign hanging from their neck saying, 'Make me feel important.' Never forget this message when working with people." It is a wonder to me that with such successful examples, so many corporations can possibly have underperforming sales departments.

Any sales representative or other independent position can continually learn from experts in their field or in other fields in order to think outside of themselves and their experience. Even one single point of view or technique or approach learned from another person can make a world of difference.

If you compare sales people with race drivers, there is actually a lot in common. It is incumbent upon the race team management to create an environment in which the racer can win. Conversely, it is incumbent on the racer to deliver the ultimate performance and seal the deal. And yet in order to perpetuate the success process, the sales person or the racer cannot claim all the glory and certainly cannot afford involving his team as part of his success. Racers do not build nor setup race cars, but no one drives like them. Sales people do not manage companies or develop products, but no one performs on the front line with the clients like they do. Sales people are the visible ones, but it is the team who wins and neither party should ever lose sight of that.

OCTANE OR OXYGEN

CHAPTER 38

What is always striking at the beginning of an endurance race is that the cars are so close that they literally form a field. Although at the start, there are only a couple of seconds from the first to the last car, by the end of the race, the winner might finish several laps ahead of the last car – quite the contrast. However, regardless of temporary results, it is essential for a racer to be able to enjoy each and every race. Enjoyment is vital in the successful pursuit of our objectives and desired results.

According to Earl Nightingale's legendary saying, "Success is the progressive realisation of a worthy ideal." A worthy ideal is what we call our vision, and its progressive realisation is what we call goals. Although they work together, they represent very different concepts. A vision is fairly holistic in that it includes your values and paradigms (beliefs). A goal is a landmark on the path to achieving that vision. Being solely focused on goals is a grave mistake that could be fatal to the realisation of the dream if you forget your vision. The reason a vision is so powerful is because it is foundationally attached to your heart's purpose, and your heart powers up your life – literally. The "heart" of a human being contains the DNA of his character and the very substance of his existence, so much so that the words "heart" and "soul" can actually be used interchangeably.

The journey of significant success can be long and tortuous at times. It will not be all about acceleration and success. When acceleration and success occur, it is always the fruit of what you have done prior to that time. Just as when you go hiking and take food along for the walk, you must make sure to have food to avoid starving your pursuit of desired results. That kind of special food is joy! Yes, you need to learn to enjoy the process, not just the attainment of it. It has been said many times that if you cannot learn to be happy on the way, you will not be happy when you get there. Artist Corita Kent spoke these famous words: **"Life is a succession of moments. To live each one is to succeed."**

World renowned motivational speaker and sales trainer extraordinaire, Zig Ziglar gives us his own personal twist on success building. *Zig* is a master of life and success fundamentals and boldly shares his faith in God as a strategic master piece of his success. One of Zig's favourite scriptures is found in Romans 8:28(NIV) **"All things work together for good, for those who love God and are called according to His purpose."** Following this wisdom we learn to develop the power of finding the good which is hidden in every difficulty. Our determination, to stay focused on the good in every situation of life truly causes us to accelerate towards our ultimate desired results. Zig once said, *"You cannot climb the ladder of success dressed in the costume of failure."* We choose our own happiness attitude; don't let others or your environment dictate which garments you should wear.

As such, we can say that happiness is a skill! Don't wait to get somewhere to be successful and be happy. Actually it is your success attitude that conditions your joy level. And your joy will become your key to making it to the destination. Learning to be happy is as important as any other skill that you will ever need to be successful.

Someone might ask, is there a happiness school? Yes there is – you are it! Assuming that you are an unhappy person, you have learned to be so. While you may feel that circumstances cause your emotions, in reality, you chose to accept that emotion and so perpetuate the miserable feelings. Helen Keller was not a racer, but she surely had the profile of a champion. The blind young girl was a world of anger in and of herself in her childhood. She could do nothing to change her blindness, but she demonstrated the courage to look outside her condition to find that her response to her condition was holding her captive, and she chose freedom. By accepting that joy and fulfilment were a decision, not a condition, she put her life on a path of discovery and truth that would leave most of us who have functioning vision totally blind in comparison. Helen Keller could have stood on the highest step of any podium as she championed our understanding of the power of the human mind.

On the search for great acceleration, we look for more octane to put into our tanks and power up our walk and achievements. Although octane is important, don't forget to mix it with the oxygen of life and joy or there will be no combustion. You may add hours to your schedule, discipline to your daily agenda, greater demands on your staff, more deadlines for your employees, or even pressure on your spouse to join in your new journey, but all of this will produce no desirable result if you cannot make room for life. Why? We are not primarily "doing machines", although we often act as though we were. We are living beings! The quality of our existence precedes our ability to produce stuff – it always takes precedent. We may at times drug ourselves with achievements, but at the end the dust will settle and we will likely experience a crisis. Every time we try to make a living and forget to make a life for ourselves and those around us, frustration, pain, and breakups are only a matter of time. If you squeeze life out of people, don't expect them to cross the finish line with you. You may boast as a survivor, but you will have failed your life or business partners in that the win was supposed to be about all of you, not just you!

Make sure that you balance demand with nurture, expectations with attention, and as you push forward on the achievement highway make use of the rest areas to relax a little. You may be tough, but not everyone has this gift; yet many can join in with you on the road to success and achievement of your true desires. Do everything in your power to not be a destroyer of individual dreams and destiny; rather, be a true leader, and become a force of hope and inspiration for others around you.

PART 8
RACING TO WIN!

QUALIFYING

CHAPTER 39

The first step in any successful race is qualifying. Qualifying is a very unique skill. Some drivers can be great racers but not necessarily great qualifiers, and vice versa. The goal of qualifying is to gain an advantage by positioning your car at the front of the starting grid. During the race, passing can prove very difficult against an opponent of similar talent and equipment. Qualifying ensures that you have the best start possible, drive in clean air and can carry that advantage into the race. There is a domino effect to qualifying. It is easy to imagine that there is a phenomenal sense of confidence that emerges from being in a pole position. You were outright the fastest against racers and teams who, like you, gave everything they had to be the best.

Good qualifying positions create a strong sense of confidence as well as a definite positive expectation for the actual race to unfold your way. That powerful combination of confidence and expectation is one of the strongest root causes of high performance and result acceleration.

As I am writing this book, news came to me of a qualifying story that encapsulates the intensity and reward of qualifying in endurance racing. The American Le Mans Series website relays the story: "In only its third event since switching to the premier LMP1 category, Drayson Racing earned its first-ever career pole position in qualifying for this weekend's Asian Le Mans Series' inaugural event at the Okayama (Japan) International Circuit. In four laps Jonny Cocker (Guisborough, Yorks, UK) piloted the No. 87 Drayson Racing Lola with Judd Power to a grid-setting lap of one minute, 19.143 seconds around the 3.7 km, 13-

turn race course. Cocker and teammate/owner Paul Drayson (London/Gloucestershire, UK) will share the Michelin tyre-shod, closed-cockpit racer in a pair of three-hour events 31 October and 1 November, which will decide the champion of the 2009 Asian Le Mans Series season."

Whilst the historic ramifications of being in the record book as the first pole winner in the Asian Le Mans Series are momentous, the importance for the unfolding racing weekend is also very significant. The championship was at stake, as well as well as an automatic invitation to the 24 hours of Le Mans in June 2010.

Against a field full of factory efforts and much more experienced prototype drivers/teams, the pole position was a significant event for the family-owned, private racing venture of Drayson Racing. Not only did it show the speed and commitment of the team but also its ability to overcome adversity. Two weeks prior, at the Monterey Sports Car Championships in Monterey, California, USA, it was questionable if the Anglo-American team would even be able to make the trip to Asia. A massive incident in which Paul Drayson was struck and pushed off course on the race's third lap caused extensive damage to the Lola Coupe. However, the team drew deep and pulled from all corners of its technical partners, including Lola Cars International and Judd Engines to prepare the car for shipment in two days. With the arrival of the car and needed parts in Japan, the crew was able to repair the No. 87 to not only survive but flourish on the first day of practice and qualifying. In your business or in your life you will experience qualifying moments, and they will be defining moments. You may have prepared for them or you may not have. Each time you can prepare for the defining moments, you will create an edge of acceleration to your results.

So how do you prepare? Well, let's look at the essential meaning of the word qualify:

1. **Creating suitability**
2. **Providing limiting and lessening restrictions**

In plain English, whether you qualify by putting some things in place or by taking others out, you are creating the perfectly tuned solution to unleash the materialisation of your desired results.

Just like in racing, you cannot qualify by just pressing the pedal to the metal. In the pursuit of your results, you cannot succeed by just pushing hard and hoping for the best. In racing, it is very important to adapt the whole car setup to the track characteristics and track conditions (fast, slow, tight corners or long curves, and wet, hot, high grip or low grip, etc.). Likewise, in life and business you must qualify your vision, or your goals, by giving serious thought to the following:

1. **Have a precise knowledge of what you want and how it fits with your environment and values.**
2. **Measure your determination to do what it takes for as long as it takes.**
3. **Asses all personal assets and skills that will help you succeed.**
4. **Have an initial plan to fill in the blanks for those areas where your assets are deemed insufficient.**
5. **Determine to be crystal clear about the above.**

Your willingness to investigate the above ideas will qualify you for the start and cause you to accelerate much faster, and it will create and keep your speed momentum. It is important to be aware that the qualifying process will not occur once and for all, but repeatedly. It is likely that it will take place many times as you come up with new ideas, strategies, and plans. Therefore it is paramount to run the qualifying round with the same commitment to best results every time. Never let complacency or yesterday's assessment provide you with the qualifying for today's race. This could lead to negative results and impair your ability to produce the acceleration that you are looking for.

GREAT START

CHAPTER 40

You have qualified well; you are now positioned favourably for a great start. You have acquired an edge over your competition. However, the qualifying glory is now gone, and it is time to unleash your acceleration power. Time to run the race. That is what you live for as a champion of life and business!

The green flag has been waved; the focus is on accelerating as fast as you can by pressing the pedal to the metal and unleashing every bit of power available to you as long as you can before the first turn comes. At this stage, it is not the time for questions and planning but rather launch and execution. This is no time for second thoughts; there is no room for hesitation, fear, or second guessing. The race is now underway.

In racing, a crash at starting time is often due to the high concentration of competition and the pressure on drivers who want to make position even before turn one – this can be risky and is not necessarily a good move. Qualifying well will position you towards the front and place you favourably to reduce the likelihood of a contact or collision right from the start.

Going back to life and business high performance, I would like to introduce you to the concepts of external and internal competition.

External competition is everything related to direct competitors outside of your circle of influence. They exist and practice in your field of endeavour or business or industry, and whether you are there or not, they will still exist, as they are not directly linked to you. Needless to say, external competition these days is incredibly tough and is inarguably a major factor in any business success. Doing everything you can to create a leading edge over your competition is a must if you intend to win! Remember that you do not have to be 50 per cent better than your competition, or even 30 per cent or 10 per cent better. The winner simply has an edge over his competitors, and that edge can be fairly small but remains an edge. Make sure that you go the extra mile in every possible dimension of your business so that you can harness the power of the leading edge.

However tough the competition is, external competition is not necessarily the hardest competition to overcome. Internal competition can be much worse, and that is not a new phenomenon but a fundamental reality. In Mark 3:24(NIV), Jesus Christ points to this: "Any kingdom divided against itself is doomed to crumble." Indeed, any infighting or any internal conflict is a major force to reckon with, as it damages the overall effectiveness of any enterprise.

The same principle applies on an individual level. Infighting or internal conflicts occur every time there is a competitive factor at play. Let's assume that you want to get control of your health and start losing weight, for example. On one hand, your desire to realise that weight loss is a qualifying force within you that empowers you to succeed. However, simultaneously you realise that you have a competing instinct acting in the opposite direction: fear of depravation has a tendency to keep you in need of more food. This will act as a counteracting force that intervenes in a diametrically opposite direction to your desire for results of weight loss and better health. This is infighting at its best: I know what I want, I can even decide what I want, but woe is me, there is another force causing me to do the very opposite of what I want. This internal conflict – just you and your conflicting desires – will actually absorb a huge amount of energy in deciding who is going to win that fight. One day you may find yourself in utter frustration and simply give up.

This is why New Year's resolutions are notoriously known as synonymous with broken promises. Any off-the-cuff decision will suffer the same demise. By making a resolution, you are simply bringing competition to a well-established system, and the battle of the wills is instantly activated. This well-established system of dissatisfying results (mix of beliefs and past experiences) is an expert in causing you frustration and has no intention of backing off. So, what are you going to do? Is there any hope? Yes, just hold on and keep reading... When you find yourself in this kind of raging race in which your desire to move forward is opposed by strong internal competition, you must sometimes back off and re-evaluate the "qualifying" position of the newcomer (the new desire and outcome you set for yourself). Is it strong enough? Is it truly a heart desire? Is it really a compelling force, or is it a mere wish without any roots that will be run over by your old way as soon as it enters the race track?

You have to decide with complete commitment that you are going to build this new reality for yourself and that you will not be told otherwise. The key word here is "decide"! Gutsy? You bet! It can even be outright scary at times. However, as your desires are well qualified (measuring your level of desire and commitment to make it happen), you will be unstoppable. Unleash your plan, stay focused, and bring aboard the leveraging force of support and possibly success-accountability partners.

According to some recent research on achievement, it appears that hearing a new idea gives you only a 10 per cent chance to succeed with that idea. However, if you prepare a plan, become accountable to another person, and follow through on it, your chances of success climb to an astonishing 95 per cent. Needless to say, there is a price to pay in this, and you will do it only if you want it badly enough. Now, as though the external and internal weren't hard enough to deal with separately, you will often be dealing with both types of competition at the same time.

A racer is constantly racing against himself internally (focus, confidence, concentration) and externally (other cars, track conditions, strategies, team dynamic), and you experience the same competition patterns in business or in relationships. For example, if you want a different relationship with your teenager, you will have to deal with the two types of competition. Your self-doubts, your lack of knowledge and confidence, and your desire for quick vindication will stand as your major internal competitors. Simultaneously, your teenage child, armed with his or her own desire for outright independence, will present major external competition to your aim to build a closer relationship. Make sure that you enter that race prepared by making a long-lasting decision to work things out. As you view all obstacles and difficulties as pure competition, not denial, you will release your hope and will for the win! You will surprise yourself when you are armed with a well-qualified desire – you will have inexhaustible force to accelerate to the finish line no matter what. And just as it is with the American Le Mans, it may be at times a gruelling endurance race, but you will race it to the end.

If you engage in a new marketing campaign, new sales effort, or new development program for your company, make sure to qualify as well as you can. Only total commitment through hard work and perseverance will allow you to blast off and create a lead over competitive forces that want to keep you from victory. Do not let that happen to you; press through, unleashing the champion within and the racer without.

ADJUSTING YOUR RACE PACE

CHAPTER 41

We just covered the subject of competition, be it internal or external, as we run the critical phase of a race from a full-out race start. However, the race is going to go far beyond turn one; actually, it can last for what seems to be an awfully long time. This is where endurance racing and the American Le Mans Series are a great representation of what "life racing" is all about. As opposed to fairly short-lived races or oval races, endurance sports-car racing takes place in a variety of complex road circuits, with multiple kinds of turns and over an extended period of time meant to test the endurance of the drivers – hence the endurance-racing terminology.

To put things in perspective, gear shifting alone can count in the thousands of upshifts and downshifts during an endurance race (19,000 to 25,000 in a 24-hour endurance race). The exercise has become a little easier in modern times with the development of sequential gearboxes and paddle shifters that eliminate the need for clutching, which can definitely be taxing for your left leg. With a conventional gearbox, not only do you operate the shifts, but you also have to create engine rpm synchronisation by heel toeing, which creates much additional work for your feet. With or without heel toeing and throttle blipping, the camera footage of race drivers' "feet dance" can create total amazement for the race fan discovering what it takes in the cockpit of a race car to create high speed.

In your drive to generate great results in your life and business, you will have to pace yourself in your racing environment. This is all about strategy. Raw speed alone never wins. Strategy is very important, and

■ RACING STRATEGIES TO CREATE HIGH PERFORMANCE

although the driver must show respectful levels of strategic capability, the race strategist in the pit lane is ultimately responsible for overall race strategy, including pace and pit stops, tire change, refuelling, and driver change. This is a complex skill set that requires a serious mix of experience and a very fine mindset, capable of administrating data to deliver the best results.

Every year the best teams compete at strategic levels. Notoriously, Audi and Peugeot fight at Le Mans for the privilege of automotive brand supremacy. More than once the slightly slower Audi defeated the Lion of Peugeot (the emblem of the company) on a strategic level. Dindo Cappello is an Audi factory driver with several Le Mans wins and American Le Mans Series LMP1 championship titles. The Peugeot 908 HDI FAP owns the overall lap record at the Le Mans, yet Dindo said, "I know our friends at Peugeot are fast, but you know the 'lion' still has to jump through the rings!" On one hand, he was joking as he referred to Audi's famed four-ringed logo. On the other hand, he was not joking at all, as Audi and the team's strategic ability have proven again and again to be nearly invincible as they have won several back-to-back wins at Le Mans. For ten solid years, they were the undefeated winners of the 12-hour Petit Le Mans (Road Atlanta, GA). This phenomenal accomplishment goes back to the launch of the American Le Mans Series in 1999. Only in 2009 did Peugeot win, after Alan McNish fell behind by spinning during a caution lap on the cold and wet track.

So how do you strategise your race and monitor your pace? You must have a superior understanding of the racing environment in which you are going to operate. You are going to need great alertness, objective analysis, and a willingness to monitor the situation. Also, you must always keep on asking good questions to lead you to the proper answers. Questions are so important that world-famous painter Pablo Picasso is even quoted as saying, "Computers are useless; they only give answers."

1. **Have you clearly formulated your vision and broken it into goals and steps?**

2. **Have you set some clear markers along the way to make sure that you are going to stay on track?**

3. Do you have enough knowledge? Do you need support?
4. Are people around you onboard? (family and/or colleagues)
5. Are those to whom you answer onboard with you? (managers/executives/board of directors)
6. Do you have a reasonable understanding of the investment in terms of time and money as well as in personal terms?

You will probably find many more questions to ask. You cannot answer all of them perfectly, and that is not a problem at all. The fact that you engage your mind in question form and that you have the discipline and commitment to answer them shows that you are serious about achieving your results; you will dramatically increase your chances to succeed.

When you are engaged in the race, the last thing you want to do is back out. So you will monitor your pace to ensure that you keep breathing throughout. Keep alert in your environment with your external and internal competition. And make sure to stop to refuel when necessary. Indeed, rest is an important part of speed, as you cannot maintain top performance when you focus continually on high speed. Since you are aiming at an overall result as opposed to top speed, give thought to your "rest" pit-stop strategy and make sure that it is part of the overall plan.

In my view, working seven days a week, 14 hours a day, is not a wise and sustainable approach. Even if you have enough energy to sustain it, unless you are a hermit, your personal life and immediate environment will take the hit of your over-commitment. This is described by Dr. John Elliot as over-motivation, and interestingly, this expert in high performance explains that it is often conducive to underachievement. So pace your race; do not become an over-motivated underachiever. Balance your approach to your results, and you will maximise the odds in your favour.

CLEAN RACING

CHAPTER 42

Now you are well into your race, you have qualified well, you have gotten off to a great start, you have survived all forms of competition, and you are definitely starting to look like you are in the groove. That is a wonderful place to be. However, the race is not over until it is over! I know that it can be annoying, but remember what makes the podium worthwhile? It is your overcoming of the challenges that you meet on the way.

Before we discuss how to race clean, let's see what happens at the opposite end of the spectrum.

In October 2009, on the hills of sunny Monterrey, CA, stretches the famous Laguna Seca race track. The final race of the 2009 ALMS was taking place there: the Monterrey Sports Car Championship. It was a unique race in more ways than one. Not only did it bring conclusion to the 2009 season, but Gil de Ferran was running the last race of his successful racing career in his beautiful Acura LMP1. Adrian Fernandez of Mexico was finding himself running what could be the last race in his Lowe's sponsored LMP2 Acura program, after a multi-year racing venture that had seen many successes. Needless to say, everyone was determined to give it their best shot and more.

The battle raged in all four classes of this emotionally charged 2009 edition. That said, there was one battle that eclipsed the others: the finish in GT2 between Jan Magnussen in the GM Corvette C6R, and Jorg Bergmeister in the Flying Lizard Porsche 997 GT3 RSR. During this epic dual, on the very last lap and in the very last turn, Magnussen and his Corvette came too hard and hit the back of the Porsche 997 of Bergmeister. The Porsche was thrown off balance and lost time on reacceleration. The Corvette sneaked in for the pass as the finish line was in sight, but the upset Porsche driver would have none of it and blocked the Corvette driver outright. The two cars were now in a drag race while banging on each other as Magnussen and his Corvette were inexorably squeezed towards the pit wall by the understandably angry Bergmeister. Magnussen kept pressing through in the very heat of the battle. Only a few yards before the finish line, his C6R spun out of control and came flying across the race track right in front of the Porsche. The result was scary and disastrous, as the Corvette violently hit the wall and tire barrier head-on creating an explosion of car parts all over the track. Porsche won, Corvette lost! Had Magnussen waited a little more, his powerful Corvette may have done the job right. By pushing hard against the back of the Porsche, he unleashed fury and lost the battle. All of his hard work was destroyed in a single manoeuvre, and any chance to win along with it.

Duals might be exciting, for racers and fans alike, but the fact remains that there is always a winner and a loser. In order to maximise your chances to win your race towards your desired results without engaging in a potentially hurtful dual against the odds, you have to focus on your best ally: the law of momentum and the virtue of continuum.

Momentum is something that you build at times and you brake at other times. Once again, this is not just a cute saying but a powerful principle that is scientifically qualified as "law". If we intend to use this law to our benefit, we must first understand it. Momentum in physics is referred to as the product of mass and velocity. They not only add up; they multiply! Every time you see multiplication, you must pay great attention, as there is great power available to gain or to lose.

The law of momentum does apply with great precision, as it is no respecter of persons or subject matter. It just is. It is written as $P = mv$, where "m" is the mass and "v" the velocity. So what good is it to you, and how will you take advantage of it?

First there is the mass aspect of mass or "Weight of Importance": it refers to the "weight" of your vision or desire or ideal. This is not a universal sense of mass, which would leave out any so-called small project. The weight of your desire means one thing: how important is it to you personally? It does not matter if you want to clean up a mess in your life or succeed as an entrepreneur. Don't fall for measuring your desire by some faulty scale of worthiness. Once again, importance to you is what matters alone. I assume of course that it is legal, moral, and ethical; otherwise you may want to think again.

As we learned before, you must condition your focus on what you want; if you become overly conscious of obstacles or competing desires or other people's input and opinions, your focus shifts to the outside, and you start losing that sense of the weight of the importance of what you are after. In racing, when you race against another race car, you may be tempted to shift your focus to the other vehicle. That is damaging, as you are not controlling the other car; you are only controlling your own. The problem here is that if you shift your focus off your own driving, your personal performance will suffer. By refocusing on your own driving, you gain greater calm and effectiveness, and you increase your chances to make the pass. Accordingly, affirm your desire to reach your goal, focus on the right course of action, be powered up by this desire, but dedicate your attention to what it takes to reach the goal – not only the goal itself!

The second aspect of the law of momentum is velocity. It refers to an applied rate of movement in a given direction. So, let's call it speed for simplicity's sake. You need direction and speed to create momentum, pretty straightforward. However, you realise here that steering in a precise direction is vital to your momentum. As for the speed itself, it is obviously created by the application of power. That power in your life and business will come from the effectiveness of your actions. We can plan all we want; execution is what will validate planning – period. At the same time, actions in and of themselves are not enough; we must take *appropriate* action. When you engage in something new, always ask yourself this question: "On a scale of 0–10, how adequate and conducive to results are my actions?" Then, on a scale of 0–10, measure your action power for every appropriate action: "Am I doing enough of what I need to do?"

In the book, *The Tipping Point*, Malcolm Gladwell explores the theory that everything is subject to a critical stage or tipping point that will accelerate you towards a specific outcome. However, once you cross over the "tipping point", your momentum starts to increase, and it becomes much harder to either slow you down or throw you off course. Everyone who has been on a bike knows that; the hard part is to gain speed to where there is enough momentum to keep you up and stable! When you think of your actions to create speed in your results, think of momentum building, think of the long-term impact of what you do, and remember that you might be closer than you think to your breakthrough success; your tipping point might be just a couple of adjustments away.

Let's bring up an important nuance: momentum and obsession are very different in nature. Although there seems to be a very fine line between them, they are not the same at all. Obsession does not care about anything but the object of obsession; momentum includes all that is necessary to reach the desired results. Obsession consumes; momentum builds up. As you arch forward in the pursuit of your desired results, ask yourself this critical question: "Am I building on the power of momentum or the power of obsession?" Both are powerful, but each will leave you with very different results. Ask yourself if you are under the impression that you are in a process of inclusion or exclusion and erosion. This will give the initial assessment of what may be at work so you can proceed immediately to the necessary adjustments.

Continuum is a mindset that applies to everything you do. It will preserve you from experiencing the well-known one step forward, two steps backwards phenomenon, which leads you away from your results. Continuum not only preserves your overall energy, it builds your confidence and develops a sense of calm in your undertakings. If you like the idea of doing more with less, let continuum be your ally.

So here you have it, the success story in full physics terms: the law of momentum. No more guesswork, no more wondering. Your destination is your desired goal, your plan is your direction, and your actions create the speed. What ties it all together is the law of momentum. Now you have a system to refer to as you build up your success speed. Even if you happen to get lost a little at times, you will see where you got off track, find where you lost momentum, and start rebuilding your impossible speed.

Let's leave the last word to Anthony Robbins: "The most important thing you can do to achieve your goals is to make sure that as soon as you set them, you immediately begin to create momentum."

PRESS IN AND TAKE IT AWAY

CHAPTER 43

When I stay with the leading pack, adjusting my race to theirs, when I am not too impatient, opportunity will present itself – this is a kairos moment – it must be seized with extreme speed of execution, almost without thinking. Many things or stages lead to this moment, or this hour, and it must be seized with absolute decisiveness.

Kairos is a Greek word for an opportune or appointed time. Kairos points to a kind of special moment in which something of an unusual nature manifests itself. Every race driver looks for such a time as this. On their professional quest to land a winning ride, the successful drivers will have to experience a kairos moment. If you doubt this, you need to know that the odds of becoming a professional race driver are 1 in 10,000. Out of this, only a handful will ever go on to become champions and win major races or championships. It can take years of committed preparation before kairos time comes into place. That is when, suddenly, wonderful things seem to come together. Success, which used to feel elusive, has finally come your way.

This could be the case when your boss tells you that you are next in line for a promotion. The same for the first big contract that you land at a new company, opening doors that you did not even dream of. Or one date that leaves you with the warm and overwhelming feeling that this time you have met someone really special with whom you would like to build your life.

Do not think of kairos as something magical in essence, but only magical in effect. There is always a powerful story that precedes a kairos moment. Opportunity will present itself to you as you prepare for it. There is a clear order when it comes to conscious decision to reach the goals that you assigned yourself. Vision, passion, determination, persistence, and diligence will always precede the forming of the kairos moment. It is called into effect when you respect the principles of sound success and fulfilment. It will simply be there for you to accelerate your results and multiply the fruit of your efforts. There may be oppositions, obstacles, and delays, but kairos will come into play.

When kairos comes, you will probably be taken by surprise. It will be there to give you the boost of acceleration that you need to propel your results forward. It may even come in unexpected form. In my thirteen-year-old son Joshua's racing career, there was a clear kairos moment that came disguised in potential tragedy. His race kart was involved in a high-speed tangle that pushed his kart sideways into the barriers and launched it airborne and inverted it, dropping my son on his head. I sincerely thank God that he landed gracefully and was not hurt. I was so glad to have invested the necessary funds in his advanced neck protector, but his motivation was badly injured. He had once more qualified well but could not turn it into results and was close to giving up.

We discussed the ordeal together and decided to pray together to find out where the opportunity was hidden in this situation. For every action there is an equivalent reaction in the opposite direction. Since trouble had clearly knocked on our door, we needed to find where opportunity was knocking as well. We found it as we made some strategic decisions about his racing equipment. We unleashed a powerful second half of the racing season, which allowed him to finish third in his class at the Canadian National Championship this year and collect several wins and virtually be on the podium at every race. Kairos had come disguised; we had to recognise it and seize the moment in its nature or miss out.

Be sure that you are alert when kairos comes and knocks at your door. Recognise what it is, and respond accordingly. If it is an opportunity presenting itself, take it. Don't think it through unnecessarily; grab it by the horns. Successful people are skilled at decision making; unsuccessful people are skilled at indecision and excuse making. Successful people can perceive and access success opportunity even when other people are distressed in the face of difficulties.

No matter where you are now, you will be given a kairos moment, a propelling opportunity. You may not be used to that experience, but be certain that kairos moments will increase in frequency and magnitude according to your willingness to respond to them. We tend to think that we know when we are ready to graduate to the next level, but God always knows when we are truly ready! Until we arrive to that point, it is crucial to follow the famous words of Sir Winston Churchill:

"NEVER, NEVER, NEVER, NEVER GIVE UP."

PART 9
RACE TEAM POWER

YOUR TEAM, YOUR WIN

CHAPTER 44

There is something truly beautiful about a successful race team. There is an energy and dedication to results that cannot leave those who witness it indifferent. There is a convergence of desires: the desire to excel and the desire to win are truly magnificent in essence. Indeed, competing and winning is a team affair; no one wins alone in car racing. Although the race-car driver is the maestro, delivering the ultimate performance, there are often dozens, at times even hundreds of people involved behind the scenes whose year-long efforts make things possible on race day.

There are many professional fields represented in a high-level racing team: design engineers, mechanics, electronic engineers, data specialists, IT professionals, administrators, marketing and public relations, finance, planning, management, logistics, and of course the famous pit crew members who will perform breathtaking tire changes and refuelling on race day.

In the area of maintenance alone, preparation for race day can go from 20 hours in entry-level racing up to in excess of 200 hours in the American Le Mans Series. For every moment of visible results, there are hundreds of steps invisible to the fans' eyes. What will stay memorable in the race would never have happened without the dedicated work of many committed people. Virtually every imaginable skill is present in a world-class race team, and on race day they must operate with the precision and reliability of a Swiss watch.

What makes superior teams is their level of preparedness in delivering superior results no matter what circumstances are thrown at them. In 2009, the Patron Highcroft Acura LMP1 race team was put to the test by the horrific crash of one of its drivers: Scott Sharp. September 23, 2010, was practice day on the hills of Road Atlanta. Victim of an apparent mechanical failure, Scott found his car suddenly oversteering beyond recovery and was left powerless in a prototype, heading furiously towards the concrete that was protected only by a couple of layers of tire barriers to absorb the impact. This kind of protection is largely sufficient when you come brushing somewhat sideways against it, but the #9 Acura was coming head-on, covering around 60 meters every second. The prototype, still rushing at speeds over 200 km/hr, propelled its driver to what was about to be a brutal and destructive impact, and at that moment nothing could be done… As Scott Sharp's car hit the tire barrier, it was instantly transformed into a cloud of flying debris.

Sharp was trapped in the carbon fibre cell, which was both his prison and his protection. Modern race cars, unlike a regular passenger car, have a highly developed inner structure that can sustain impacts of over 100 G force. These cells can sustain high energy-dissipating deformation and yet preserve the space around the driver in order to protect him. Scott Sharp's Acura came to a stop on the grass, totally unrecognisable, and as everyone stopped breathing in suspense, the driver emerged unscathed out of what was left of his destroyed prototype.

The survival and casual walk away of Scott Sharp was stunning and wonderful, but something else extraordinary was about to happen. As the car was being removed from the track, the Highcroft race team was preparing its response. They had a choice of withdrawing from the race, which was going to take place 24 hours later, or rebounding from the disaster. Of all 4,000 parts of the prototype, the Acura was only 10 per cent salvageable, which I am sure you will agree is not much. However, Highcroft, under the leadership of its owner Duncan Dayton, a highly successful racer himself, decided to rebuild the car in time for the race. Never before had an on-site reconstruction attempt been made with such magnitude of destruction.

■ RACING STRATEGIES TO CREATE HIGH PERFORMANCE

Rebuilding a race-ready LMP1 car in 24 hours was not conceivable in most people's minds, but Highcroft mobilised all of its skill and motivation and, as one, the team went to work. A new "tub", the central part of the car that protected Scott Sharp from an otherwise fatal crash, was flown in, as were many other parts. The team concentrated all of its efforts and tapped into its planning capabilities to successfully have the car back on track within 24 hours, and they succeeded. In an organised ballet, the team engineers operated with incredible speed and efficiency to assemble the car around the engine, including all suspensions, gearbox assembly, electrical, telemetry, hydraulics, electronics, and other systems. Thanks to their preparedness, their high degree of professionalism and commitment, as well as their unshakable dedication to results, they succeeded where no one had ever ventured before.

Highcroft is the epitome of the ultimate world-class race team. However, their recipe for success is neither unique nor impossible to replicate. Yes, they had the funding for their enterprise, yet no amount of funding will ever buy the spirit of a company. The spirit of a company is at the root of all of its achievements and will be formed over an extended period of time by high-quality, committed leadership. It comes from clear communication, effective training, and an extra-mile approach. This kind of performance does not come out of self-preservation but from a passionate and diligent engagement to win.

Whoever wants to win, particularly in our new soft economy, cannot lack in the area of team performance. Whether you work from home, own a small business, or carry corporate responsibility, you must harness race team power to successfully carry out your objectives.

Racing, because of its high intensity, rapidly singles out passivity and non-cooperation. On a race team, no one works only because he or she needs a job and a pay check. The line-up to get into a great team is too long for half-hearted people to make it in. You cannot fake passion, you cannot fake commitment, and you cannot pretend excellence. The pressure is too intense in the racing world for any form of complacency.

If you are in business for yourself, make sure to surround yourself with "like-minded" people who will strive with you and partner with you in a common and cross-contributing dynamic. There is no need to do it all yourself. You have probably heard it many times: "Don't reinvent the wheel!" Don't fight every battle either. Accelerate your results by leveraging others' input and influence. As you work with other people, the goal is to increase a common momentum; yours as well as theirs.

It will be critically important that you be on the same page as your team through competent communication. Otherwise, you might be disappointed to realise that what seemed to be a primary objective has become a secondary pursuit. Simply be forthcoming by asking your partners why they want to work with you, what a successful result looks like to them, and if they are ready to give their very best efforts. And be certain to reciprocate in the same terms that you expect from them.

Teamwork in any corporation is paramount and reflects directly on the overall results of the company. Tragically, like so many critical missions of a company, teamwork can be labelled as something we have to do and sort of put up with. Any company that is stuck in the impasses of dysfunctional teamwork must make it a priority to "shock its heart" back to life. Like any other principle, it must be known and respected, not pushed aside to the benefit of policies and procedures. When teamwork becomes a feature or a burden and not a foundation, trouble is lurking ahead.

When teamwork is broken, it is most likely that external intervention will be needed as the bridges of communications have been damaged and trust is badly wounded. External input will be able to facilitate a renewing of relationship dynamics as the focus can be directed towards solution, not dominance and vindication. As in so many cases, the shift must be redirected from "who is right" to a more constructive "what is right".

How about in a family or in a marriage? Are there teamwork dynamics there? My wife Jo Anne seems to think so. She has an incredible passion for family and parenting and speaks on these subjects. She gives parents access to critical knowledge for creating quality relationships with their children. The first step, like for any other team, is that a family requires a clear identity that people can be attracted to.

Our family established that early on through a family mission statement. Interestingly enough, we recently found our mission statement in a box, where it must have been stored when it was taken off the wall during some house remodelling. Jo Anne and I were amazed to discover that the principles that we had laid out consciously some years ago were in full swing in our family life today, even though we had not read the statement in a long time.

Once a strong family identity is established, it becomes easier to gage parenting in respect to your family brand! At this point in time, we are about to rework our family mission statement, as we believe that it is time for our children to give their input. They are now mature enough to have a say in it and make it their own as well.

A "race-team mindset" of passion, cohesiveness, and desire to go for the win is fully applicable to any team. It is up to the leadership to be willing to do so. Make the decision, regardless of your own team dynamics, to create a winning spirit, and harness the power and edge of powerful teamwork. You will accomplish so much more with so much less pain; the race-team mindset is a powerful result accelerator!

TEAM LEADERSHIP

CHAPTER 45

Racing is about superior control skills: you constantly strive to steer the race car in a given direction, and you also create a dynamic input by proactively projecting and adjusting what will cause it to perform at its best. In race driving, over-controlling, or under-controlling – which is also called reacting – will inevitably lead to loss of performance, and the same applies to all of us as we are piloting our lives and businesses.

The subject at hand is the quality of your leadership, no matter what you are leader of – be it your family or your business. The components and the skills required can vastly vary; however, in essence, the nature of your leadership remains the same. Do you lead by demand, do you lead by fear, do you lead by need, or do you lead by inspiration? All forms of leadership can produce some results, but there are certain leadership traits that can create much greater results.

Albert Schweitzer, the famous German medical missionary and Nobel Prize winner once said, *"Example is not the main thing in influencing others. It is the only thing."* Are you willing to go first and pave the way for the results that you want to see? Demanding what you are not willing to give yourself is a sure recipe for difficulties and potential disaster. Do everything in your power to be an inspiration to others by first being a living example of the things that you want to see happen around you. Want more effective communications? Go first. Want more cooperation between team members? Go first. Want more respect from your spouse? Go first!

RACING STRATEGIES TO CREATE HIGH PERFORMANCE

Hold on, you may say, I have already done my part, but people around me are not responding. Well, although that is possible, it is highly unlikely. Let me illustrate.

As you are strapped into your race car and running some fast laps, you decide to push the envelope and go even faster, looking for additional performance. Understanding that you are the one who is going to create this extra speed and performance, you narrow your focus, unleash your will and skills, and brilliantly push the car to its limit – and suddenly it loses control under you, and you crash.

Who crashed? You or the car? I believe you did; the car was the victim of your leadership, not vice versa. If you disagree with that, then next time you sit in your car you will have to admit that it is in charge of you – not a nice place to be. When you take control of something through leadership, you have to assume the responsibility all the way through, no matter what happens. Although it may feel at times as though you are betrayed by the vehicle with which you are working, you still have to take responsibility for it. When you push people beyond their current state of performance, no matter what it is – good or bad, you have to make sure that you understand their limits. And if those limits are a problem, you will be responsible for working on that with them first before you can ask them to embrace your leadership. No one said that leadership was always fair or easy.

We too often make the fundamental mistake of confusing leadership and position. You have position by appointment, but you exercise leadership by virtue and skills. Being in a position confers rights, but leadership calls for responsibilities. The assumption that we are automatic leaders because we have a position, be it in marriage or in a company or in owning a business, is a grave mistake. Our understanding is that we ought to grow our leadership to serve the position, and not use our position to ensure leadership. If you can see the difference, you will probably find a huge runway for growth, a wide-open track ahead of you. If you don't, you will probably spend an awful lot of time on the pit lane trying to figure out what is not working, and irritatingly enough, you will most likely never find the solution that you are looking for.

Being a true and effective leader is a personal issue before a functional issue. In the whole range of issues that leadership can cover, from family to business to large corporations, make sure that you are first and foremost a diligent example who will allow people to follow you as they find in you the inspiration to power up their own journey.

Stephen R. Covey packs a wonderful punch line on leadership by example when he says: *The "Inside-Out" approach to personal and interpersonal effectiveness means to start first with self; even more fundamentally, to start with the most inside part of self / with your paradigms, your character, and your motives. The inside-out approach says that private victories precede public victories, that making and keeping promises to ourselves precedes making and keeping promises to others. It says it is futile to put personality ahead of character, to try to improve relationships with others before improving ourselves.*

This makes a world of difference and sets apart the leaders from the simple pushers. Leaders inherit results; pushers inherit turmoil and chaos. I know which one will best create impossible speed in my results, and I am sure that you do too.

TEAM COMMUNICATIONS

CHAPTER 46

You will notice on the race track that virtually everyone on the race team is wearing radio communication equipment. They are interconnected to a central communication system. The obvious reason here is that the noise level is so high that you could not possibly expect to be heard effectively without the noise reduction headsets with built-in radios. The other reason is that team members, which of course includes the driver in his car, are scattered in different positions in the pit area and on the race track and yet need to maintain contact. While this may seem obvious to anyone who has ever watched racing, it is imperative to understand that when the obvious need for communication is not met, the next obvious thing takes place: big problems.

As Gil de Ferran and his Acura LMP1 were experiencing gearbox hydraulic problems at Mosport in 2009, he had no way to relay his intentions to come in to his pit crew, as the radio in the car was failing as well. The team jolted as they saw their car suddenly veer off the track and head for the pits. It was early in the race, Gil had been driving spectacularly, and they were leading and not expecting that change of course. Panic set in as Gil de Ferran started to get out of the car in an attempt to combine the stop with a driver change, which was equally unannounced. The co-driver, the young French rising star Simon Pagenaud, was not even around, and the crew frantically waved Gil de Ferran to get back in the car and buckle up again, and to include all radio connections. They re-injected some hydraulic fluid into the gearbox, but needless to say, the overall manoeuvre was not effective for the team results. They were the same world-class team they had always been, but for a brief period in time, as radio communications broke down, the team's functional cohesiveness was incapacitated. Unfortunately, what is a brief moment in other circumstances becomes a dreadfully long time in racing, as minutes feel like hours.

The same happens for any company or any relationship in which communications have broken down at an inopportune time. Problems quickly compound as the link of common understanding is missing, and this causes people to react inappropriately or ineffectively as everyone is trying to figure things out. From a potential standpoint, we have a certain amount of energy and time to use in any given day. When energy and time are devoted to figuring out why our communications are dysfunctional, be it with our company or our family, our productive time can be vastly diminished.

Do people around you really know where you are heading, what you expect of them, and what you are committed to give them in return? Do you tend to inspire, motivate, and empower people around you, or do you just throw a large "trust me" blanket over everyone? The trust factor can work for a little while, but unless effective and high-performance communication are actively in place, it is unlikely that you will reach your destination. Even to yourself, you must clearly express your mission, vision, values, and goals if you are to accomplish what you want. If it is critical that you communicate with yourself, you can appreciate how much more important and complex it is to communicate with others involved in your life or your business.

William Arthur Ward, an American scholar, wrote: "Before you speak, listen." In high-performance communications, make listening a priority over speaking. Everyone would naturally agree with this principle, yet our need to be right, our tendency to look for a solution even before we know what the problem is, defies this very principle. We tend to make every effort to be understood, and yet we do not have any practical approach to listen first.

Listening is a heart attitude that finds priority in hearing what is important to another person. By nature I am racer; let me win first, and then I will listen. I learned at great expense to myself and to those around me that this is not how things work for maximum results. I came to realise that my self-centeredness on the subject is rooted in impatience, which is rooted in insecurity – ouch! Every confident leader can actively and constructively listen and make room for expressed opinions, even if they vastly differ from his or her own. High-performance communication creates a profound sense of belonging and promotes trust and confidence. When people are not confident, it is related to their perception of their own value. Listening is the beginning of building confidence. When this is in place, you can start giving of your acceleration knowledge for greater results. Just as no one enters a room without first opening the door, we must receive express permission or establish a relationship before communicating our own views.

Any great racer has a feel for his or her car. There is a bond between man and machine; there is a knowing of what is going on. This kind of feeling is part of effective communication. No, I am not telling you to ask your car to speak back to you! I am pointing to the fact that listening is not necessarily just about words; it is often expressed in feelings. For some people, this kind of listening is still to be developed. This is, however, the most powerful form, the unsaid and the unexpressed. If you can perceive it, you will be an amazing leader, because you will be able to read between the lines and express fruitful results as you build strong bonds of collaboration.

Whatever modes of communication are used – auditory, visual, or on the basis of feelings – they have to be highly developed in your life and your organisation. Always remember that listening is not so much something you do as it is a decision to make it a priority. Somehow it is connected to who you really are. You don't do "listening"; you are a listening person or you are not. The good news is that even if you are not, you can choose to become one!

EVERYONE COUNTS

CHAPTER 47

Racing illustrates brilliantly that results are directly dependent upon these little things that we can easily overlook, categorise as small, and judge as unimportant. High performance in racing allows us to gain a helpful understanding of the tremendous importance of small things. Indeed we come to realise that small is not synonymous of insignificance or unimportance. There are many small things in our lives and our business that hold the keys to great success.

First let's look at what happens during a pit stop. We will look briefly at Formula 1 and American Le Mans, which have very different rules for pit stops and yet arrive at the same realities.

Normal scheduled pit stops have fairly simple and straightforward objectives: tire changes and fuel fill-up plus light maintenance or aerodynamic adjustments if necessary. Fuel fill-up is fairly simple: put the nozzle in the hole and release the fuel. You probably do this every week for your own car. Of course, tire change is one of the most basic manoeuvres on any car: remove the nuts, remove the wheel, insert the new wheel, insert back the nuts, and tighten. Small stuff, isn't it? However, when you have to do all this in under ten seconds – less time than it takes to pour your cup of coffee with cream and sugar – then things start to change a little! Now what seemed to be a small thing is a major thing, because in the search of speed of execution, the difficulty skyrockets.

In Formula 1, during those ten seconds typically over 20 people will have performed their assigned role in perfect harmony and synchronisation: four wheels will have been replaced, gas-tank refuelling will have been completed, a visual inspection of the car will have been performed, the driver's visor will have been cleaned, and the aero will have possibly received some adjustments; all this in under ten seconds. Little things like tripping over the hose, having a wheel nut resist a little, the driver stopping two inches too far and hitting the front man with the jack, and the tenths of a second start building up against your pit stop. If your car gets back on track with a 0.5 second delay (about a blink of an eye), it is enough to create a handicap of six or seven car lengths! This in itself could cost your driver the outcome of the race in a very tight fight. Yes, a blink-of-an-eye difference on small tasks now has enormous consequences.

In Lexington, Ohio, on July 20, 2008, a pit stop was about to take place during Mid-Ohio American Le Mans Series Grand Prix. The #66 Acura LMP1 was completing its scheduled pit stop with Simon Pagenaud at the wheel. The car was released prematurely, as the refueler had not fully disengaged the nozzle from the car. Removing a fuel nozzle is a small thing, but it became a very important thing as the car pulled away with the nozzle attached to it, and fuel spread all around the refueler. Tragically for Keith Jones, who was holding the nozzle that particular day, the fuel ignited, and Keith was badly burnt. Although he has been back racing with the team, demonstrating the undeterred motivation and character of true champion, he bears the marks for the rest of his life for that small thing that went wrong.

You may think of your role at work as a small thing, but I invite you to not consider it unimportant. If you are a manager in your organisation, you may see some assignments or work positions as small things, yet they may be critical to the overall performance of your department. You may think that the little things you do every day, like taking the time to kiss and hug your family goodbye, are too small to be bothered with, but are they? You may be doing pretty well in life except for those more elusive parts of your existence, which after all are not a big deal – but are they? How many emotions have we kept inside, unexpressed and festering within, brushing them aside as small and unimportant?

Your life may have nothing to do with racing and its extreme conditions. Although the consequences of your way of handling the small things may not be visible instantly, there is no way that they will not have an impact on your results over the long term, because small is often very important.

Make the decision to open your eyes to little things and give them the consideration of what they might be able to contribute to your high-performance results. You may be blown away when you realise the importance and the power of the little things in building the results you want.

Raymond Aaron of Toronto, Ontario, is a long-time coach who runs a millionaire mentoring program; you can call it a millionaire school. Mr. Aaron talks very eloquently about the power of messes: "Every mess is a lock on the door of abundance." Now he does not speak about the size or perceived importance of the mess. It can range anywhere from a messy desk to messy finances, messy relationship or nutrition, messy prospecting in your sales, or messy reporting in your organisation. How about messy thoughts? Do you know that fear and worries are messy thoughts? They create havoc but do not solve anything. Every time anything is out of sorts and turning into a state of disorganisation and chaos, it is a mess. Every mess reduces our ability to prosper. It is not that we cannot accumulate more, but we have countless messes weighing on our pursuit of more in our lives and business. Each and every one of them, even the smallest, partake in slowing our progress. Because messes are expressions of what we know goes on inside of us, they dictate our results.

So let's go on a mess hunt! This will cause you to skyrocket in your overall awareness, sense, and effectiveness about controlling your life and direction. Too often, it is not big things that hold us back, but a multitude of little things that we have let invade our lives and creep up on our results. Put a stop to it and regain control, and harness the power of managing those things that you used to call small. They may be very important and critical to your success.

Of all messes, the most important ones are team messes. Team-wide messes create team-wide damage. Once again, they most likely have crept up insidiously over the course of time through small mismanagement issues, or they have been allowed outright through the entrance of small things. After all, who should worry about small things? We have some more important things to do. Who should worry about those who are not good producers in your organisation? Let's focus on the best and everything will be alright, you might say...

Some of you may have heard of the law of Pareto; it is also referred to as the 80/20 rule – 80 per cent of your results come from 20 per cent of your activities. This very helpful model allows us to prioritise our actions for what really makes a difference and creates results. What this does not imply is that 80 per cent of what has to be done can be left undone. Rather, it should be managed and possibly delegated, because it cannot be neglected. Focusing on our priorities, although essential to high performance, does not call for negligence of the rest. Otherwise, leaving too many small things undone or unfinished will soon create a big mess that cries out to be addressed.

Hopefully, after reading this chapter you will think differently about disregarding the small stuff. Beware of falling victim to the pendulum effect and becoming consumed with the little to the point of missing out on the big picture. This approach also leads to a lack of results because busyness replaces effectiveness. The importance of the small is always to be viewed in the context of maximising your results, not of paralysing your course with details.

From now on, recognise that the smallest contributions can have great importance and that everything has its place. Take the time to acknowledge the value of those who live or labour with you. Go beyond the obvious towards the more subtle and powerful dimension of what can seem small at first glance. What is small to you can be a big affair for your children or highly important to your team members.

Think big and be conscious of the small – therein may lie the key to the abundance you have been looking for.

PART 10
SETTING UP FOR RACE DAY

DATA ANALYSIS

CHAPTER 48

Once you have integrated many of the impossible-speed concepts into your life, one of the most important ongoing tasks you must still undertake is the monitoring of your acceleration path to your desired results. Today is race day, execution day, high-performance day, and reality check! When race day arrives, it is time for everything you have prepared for to come display its actual results.

How do you know how you are doing? How do you gage your evolution and your overall performance? What system do you use for feedback on your state of affairs? Whether you think you are doing great, or whether you think you are not, how do you measure where you are at?

On any road car, sets of gages and instruments are designed to make visible and readable what might otherwise be invisible to the naked eye. This translates into interpretable data, and we are going to look now at two types of data – critical data and performance data.

Critical data is a form of basic information just to make sure that everything is running smoothly. You have some of these systems on your own car such as: speed indicator, engine rpm, engine temperature, oil pressure and temperature, and many others. Without them you would be driving blind and could not run your vehicle in proper conditions.

It is interesting to note that modern cars are so sophisticated and reliable that we often take for granted their amazing capabilities. An average combustion engine contains hundreds of moving parts in constant motion, with pistons travelling up and down 50 to 100 times per second while being constantly ignited with fuel, creating controlled explosions! Did you ever think that when you cruise on the highway at 2,000 rpm, your V6 engine is producing 12,000 explosions per minute? All the while you are enjoying music, sipping your favourite coffee, and talking to your passengers, or making a hands-free phone call in a temperature-controlled environment and relaxing in a comfortable seat.

Unassumingly, we pack our days with extreme busyness, push ourselves to the limit constantly, and when the warning lights come on, we shut them down with temporary countermeasures or quick fixes. When we are fatigued we get an energy bar, when in pain we get painkillers, when illness manifests we get some drugs, and even when depression imposes its debilitating force we find a medical treatment. What would happen if we were to consider all these symptoms as warning lights on the dashboard? Would you pluck out a warning light with a screwdriver when it comes on in your car, or would you try to find the underlying issue? Yet when our bodies and minds give us warnings, we push them aside and ignore them in a bid to just keep going. But ultimately, we will pay the price.

When it comes to anyone's life, there will be times when circumstances are difficult. We have a signal telling us that some part of our life is suffering. If you just try to hide the problem, ignore it, or "quick fix" it, you are in danger of making it worse. You must find the root cause that is behind that situation.

We must learn to read our life signals properly and respond adequately by readjusting our schedule or priorities and, if necessary, by removing the energy-draining activities as we choose to seek life-affirming activities. How about cutting off some news or TV time and instead try exercising or cooking or spending time outdoors with our kids or friends, or learning new skills, or contributing to our favourite charity – or any of the endless of things we might enjoy? We all have 24 hours a day, but what we do with it makes a world of a difference. Some build their lives, others burn them out, while some people, sadly, outright waste them. If you are experiencing some warnings on your life dashboard, don't wait – respond quickly by doing what will accelerate you in the direction of your results, not away from them. Like any form of navigation, life navigation requires quick and frequent corrections, which are much easier than occasional big corrections possibly in response to crisis. Stay alert and respond as fast as you can.

In business, the situation is fairly similar by virtue of human factors. You have to learn to read the warning signals. If you are losing your employees, this is not only a problem but also a data feedback that something is running out of order. In a recent interview, William Green, Chairman and CEO of Accenture, which employs 177,000 people, put it this way: *If you look at why people in general leave companies, they leave because they get bored. High-performance people are learners by nature. And as long as they are learning, they will stay where they are.* Consider what core problems might result in resignations and give them answers of human dimension. Systems are important, but they will not necessarily inspire motivation in people. Mr. Green continues: *There are companies that are just sort of stuck where they are, and they like the status quo. In the end, that's the difference between winners and losers in corporate America and around the world. That's the contract. So, the question is, how do you get motivated learners? So, I bring this back to me, and ask how did I become a motivated learner? Somebody inspired me!*

Once again, inspiration is connected to our heart's desire, to our blueprint for success, to our values and motivations, to our skill and talents. That is why inspiration is central to developing high performance.

As you aim at the world of high performance, you need more than a warning system; you need comprehensive data feedback. The race engineers work in concert with the driver to get the best feedback possible regarding the car performance on a given day. This is used in turn to maximise the setup of the vehicle in specific race conditions and to allow it to perform at its best. There is a general feedback from the driver, telling how the car behaves. We will look in the next chapter at the fascinating analogy of a tight car (difficult to turn) or a loose car (has a tendency to overturn and lose grip at the back) as well as many other nuances relating to handling and engine performance.

The other kind of detailed feedback is going to come to the pit lane while the car is on track with live telemetry. Dozens of parameters are simultaneously charted in order to define the role of each one in the overall equation of performance as the car progresses on the track. An American Le Mans prototype will typically be equipped with various gages measuring in real time the accelerations to which the car is subject: be it vertically, laterally, or longitudinally. Knowing the intrinsic performance of each assembly or component and possibly understanding its interaction with the others is vital to creating very high levels of speed and performance.

Generally speaking, we have little ability to effectively monitor human behaviour; certainly we cannot do it remotely like we do with machines. Nonetheless, we understand from this connection between data feedback and high performance that we cannot expect very high performance in our lives and business without some significant equivalents.

As you move towards high-performance results in life and business, you must graduate in your level of awareness and understanding of your own behaviour. This is easier said than done. However, there are a few clear pointers that may indicate a need for your attitude "setup" adjustment for maximised performance.

Do you ever find any of the following?

1. **You procrastinate instead of taking action**
2. **You talk before you think**
3. **You cave in under pressure**
4. **You reset your goals when it gets too tough**
5. **You react more than you respond to any challenging situation**
6. **You feel afraid more often than you feel confident**
7. **Your thoughts are not "under control"**
8. **Your emotions undermine the achievement of your goals**

9. You think more about the liabilities of the past than the possibilities of the future
10. You lose your temper when provoked
11. You focus on negative outcomes
12. You experience repetitive patterns of failure
13. You cannot pass the "fantasy" level of your dreams and feel stuck when acting upon your ideas

I could list many more, but all of these are performance data feedbacks. They are not sentencing judgements; they just give you a simple performance measurement. If you want change, you have to implant new truths that will replace these unsupportive systems. For example, if you identify that you have a quick temper and would like to change your setup, write on paper the affirmation of the new result that you want for yourself. "Today I choose to develop a new attitude. I will develop poise and control day after day. I decide to not be easily provoked, and I will listen before I speak. I will take criticism constructively and not react. If I fail and get angry, I will come back to this truth and try again. I choose to adjust my setup for maximised performance and regain control of my emotions right now."

If you have had difficulty arriving at the results you want by yourself, don't give up. I encourage you to get the assistance of a professional coach to help you develop these areas and to get you accelerating towards your results. However, never fall for the low-speed version of your "character setup" which usually declares: "That is just the way I am!" Replace that with the racer syntax for success: "That is the way I currently function, but I am going to progressively transform these performance areas so that I can achieve my true desires and succeed in all of my endeavours!"

OVERSTEERING, UNDERSTEERING

CHAPTER 49

As you may remember, in chapter three we discussed entry and exit corners representing the types of decisions you will need to make – exit corner: holding back (long-term effect), or entry corner: fast decisions (short-term opportunity). This addressed the nature of the decision or, its racing equivalent, the nature of the turn that the driver has to negotiate with maximum speed. What it did not address is the setup of the car to best handle these types of corners. We will now look at the human equivalent of setup for high performance – your behaviour.

Before we can progress, you need to know that, generally speaking, any car has either an understeering or oversteering tendency. It gets much more complicated in real racing, but for our purpose, let's focus on the two main traits – understeer and oversteer – and first define them:

Understeer or "tight": tendency to turn less than desired – pushes away from the apex and towards the outside of the corner with loss of front-end grip.

Oversteer or "loose": tendency to turn more than desired – tends to slide towards a spin with overall loss of grip particularly on the rear end.

You might be an understeerer: a cautious and steady individual who has a hard time making direction changes or adapting to a changing environment. Or you might be an oversteerer: primarily enthusiastic, who easily makes decisions and embraces change but possibly lacks a little traction on the corners when the time comes to accelerate and move forward. It is important to know that both are useful, both have strengths and weaknesses, and ultimately, both are enormously needed. The secret, however, lies in learning how to set it up to maximise the benefits for your life and your business.

People can dynamically adapt their behaviours to any conditions that they encounter. The mindset of "take me as I am" is not a very advanced solution as it clearly shows a person who is not even willing to try. You could compare it to a race car out of the box that is never set up or adjusted for any track condition – not a winning solution. In race-car development terms, it is outright unthinkable. This kind of attitude might work well in some conditions, but it would be disastrous in others, leaving you with an overall "low-level" performance score! We have been given the ability to function beyond instinct, into the reality of dynamic behaviour. Dynamic behaviour is not to be confused with high energy. Dynamic refers to our power to adapt to our circumstances while staying on course to reach our desired results and arrive at our desired destination. We have the ability in any situation, as many times per day as necessary, without running out of steam, to direct our behaviour in a way that is structured for maximum results.

We can move from reactive behaviour into responsive dynamic behaviour at will. If you want high-performance results, you need responsive or dynamic behaviour. In reactive behaviour, the person is a victim of circumstances. In responsive behaviour, the person decides to make the most of those circumstances to the point of influencing them in a spirit of leadership. Quite the contrast, isn't it?

I must confess that too often, I find myself caught in reactive behaviour. Do you get angry when criticized or unfairly treated? Do you feel hopeless when things do not work your way? Do you constantly lose your temper with your children? Do others' opinions matter more than your own understanding of yourself? Do you find refuge in addictive substances of any kind? Do you find yourself lonely and out of touch with people around you? If you say yes to any of these – you are functioning at a reactive level. In simple terms, you are letting your environment shape your experience of life and your beliefs about yourself and your life.

Consider upgrading your response level. But what does this look like? When bad news comes to you, you will immediately look for the opportunity to strengthen your resolve to move forward. When someone pushes your buttons, you will not be affected to the point of losing control of your emotions. There is a big difference between being sensitive to people's input and being vulnerable to criticism. You will know that your peace is related to your state of heart, not to external conditions. You may lack money, but you deploy new strength and creative thinking to find more. People don't recognise your talents, but you still love them and seek those who will. You lose a job, but you say thank you for the opportunity to find another one, better than the one before.

This happened to me right after moving to Canada. I lost my first position after three months, as the airline that I was working for went into receivership and was later acquired by the competition. Was I initially affected by the news? More than that, I felt like I had been run over by a semi truck; I felt totally let down and was angry at the management. But I felt like God reminded me through this that there was a lot more available for me if I were to let go of my fear reactions and welcome a new opportunity through responsive expectation. I got another position within a month with a 33 per cent increase in salary. As time goes on, I still see ups and downs; however, the land of opportunity is getting larger and larger as I am willing to humble myself and find energy for new sets of actions in the firm hope that there is always more in store for me if I am willing to respond in expectation and not react negatively to my circumstances. It is not how strong you are or how fair the situation is; it is how you will choose to respond.

Steven R. Covey, international leadership expert, said, "Between stimulus and response, there lies our freedom." So what are you going to do when the next turn comes at you more or less unexpectedly? I trust that you will choose response over reaction and will determine which behaviour is most suited to this situation. Be totally committed to finding what value you can draw from the situation. Dynamically adapt yourself and enjoy the "unfair advantage" provided by the power of choice, and create a competitive edge that even the most advanced race prototypes on the American Le Mans circuit will never have.

THE CIRCLE OF GRIP

CHAPTER 50

As a car races on the track, the contact patch of the tire that is the actual area in contact with the track will offer the car a certain grip envelope. The art of race driving will include the ability to exploit the maximum grip within that circle. For example, if you are braking at the limit of locking your wheels, you do have maximum deceleration, but there is virtually no extra grip capability to generate a turn. Should you maintain that maximum effort of braking and turning simultaneously, you would exceed the circle of grip and lose control of the car, with its typical screeching sound and big black marks on the asphalt. The same applies for all kinds of combinations of forces as you pilot your race car at the edge of its performance.

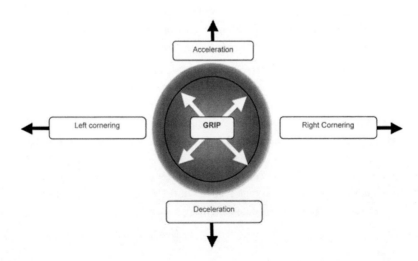

within their own circle of grip! You probably have experienced this already; when you try to push to the max in every direction – just like the race driver, you will lose control. Sometimes you can push pretty hard, which may make you think that you will be fine. However, like the race driver, you will experience crossing over the limit of your own grip; a little extra pressure and you are off! You find yourself spinning at high speed and out of control. You jump on the brakes to bring things to a stop with your tires screeching and smoking! You cannot see anything, you don't know what to do, and you are bracing for the impact because you know that you are about to crash. You realise that you will not make the deadline that you promised your client, or you will not be able to honour your commitment to your family, and it might be one time too many.

Being out of control is a horrible situation and should be avoided at all cost. If you ever find yourself coming near the edge of available grip or exceeding your limits, it may not be too late to operate a prompt correction. First you must take a good look to see where your energy is being employed and possibly dissipated. From there you can do two things: increase the grip or lessen the efforts.

Increasing the grip is finding support or counsel outside of yourself and your circle of relationships. If you cannot hire more people or the services of a consultant or a counsellor, then plan on downsizing your efforts in order to regain control of the situation at home or at work. But please realise that where your life or business has exceeded the limit of grip, you must reset the model. That is very important; things will not change on their own or clean themselves up. Remember that you are the one driving, and don't let the car drive you – because you know what will happen if you do that.

If necessary, pull into the pit lane, gather the crew, study the problem, order the replacement parts, fix it all up, and get ready to enjoy your new ride after the repairs are done! Yes, everything can be totally renewed or even transformed if you are willing to put the proper work and effort into it, but you have to really want it. And if this is something very valuable to you, like your marriage, your children, your career or finances, you may have to spend some extra time, and it may even require a financial investment to find the solution. However, if it is what you really desire with all your heart, you will see it come to pass.

From a high-performance point of view, if you are not producing the results you need, your system is simply not providing you the traction required. You may lack grip in the form of either a lack of knowledge or a lack of supportive environment. Or you may have the necessary grip available, but you are going to have to push a little harder to exploit the grip limit and accelerate faster through specific actions that will lead you to your desired results at impossible speed. Remember that very often, maximum performance is not in total reform of plans, but in significant and relevant adjustments that are conducive to maximum results.

My experience in the business and sales fields has shown me that there are some definite characteristics and statistical ratios in every business. If you need to prospect 100 people to get one sale, you will not get any results until you pass the "99" level, even though you worked hard to get there. To make matters worse, things are not consistent over short periods of time, so only the overall view of statistics tells the true story. But once you know the story, if you are not willing to respect it, your results will suffer the consequences. Knowledge of the specific condition in which you operate is essential to create high performance. The exciting part is that you can find it if you start approaching your work like a race team approaches race-car performance. Aim at maximum feedback and data management, and control every parameter that you can. Then the driving will be much more pleasant.

Thinking in terms of available grip takes away any unsupportive self-judgement and condemnation. It is not about being good or bad, but about learning to manage what we can do. It teaches about timing and procedures. The book of Proverbs in the Bible says that "there is a time and a procedure for everything" (Prov. 3:1). This kind of knowledge and understanding will allow you to make maximum use of your life or business circle of grip and avoid waste or burnouts.

The amazing thing about our available circles of grip is that when we master them, they tend to grow bigger. That is good news – you are not limited to your current level of performance. Call it growth or maturity, if you will, but the truth is that as we prove ourselves in handling the smaller things with high performance, the next step up is already on the horizon.

Start thinking today about everything you do in the context of your available circle of grip, and discover how greatly and effectively you can accelerate your results. And believe me, high performance is somewhat addictive; you will never go back!

SPEED OR DOWN FORCE

CHAPTER 51

Everything contains an equivalent in the opposite direction. When it comes to aerodynamics, there is one continual dilemma in design and setup. Every time you add down force to increase the grip of the car by loading it aerodynamically, you also generate drag, which slows the car down. In life and business, wisdom and discernment will cause you to determine the best functional compromise. You will soon come to realise that no matter which ideal you strive for, everything is a matter of compromise. Do not let your heart sink at the news, because that is a good thing – why? Because it takes two opposite forces to create control towards desired results.

The best race cars, and particularly the beautiful and highly advanced Le Mans prototype (LMP), are amazing machines that are the fruit of enormous amounts of design, manufacturing, and development. Prototype manufacturers like Lola, Radical, Zytech, Oreca, and of course Acura, Audi, Peugeot, and Porsche all make use of advanced computer-assisted designs to develop the best car. A scale or full-scale model is built for wind-tunnel testing. This allows them to determine the car's aerodynamic characteristics. A massive propeller forces air into the tunnel where the car is solidly attached. Various methods like probes, smoke, and even little wool tufts are used to measure and visualise the behaviour of air mass on and around the car.

Generating down force throughout the car without an unreasonable amount of drag and turbulence has been and will be a never-ending quest of all race-car designers and teams – even as we progress forward. Progress raises the levels of challenges but does not take them away.

As you work at your own high-performance setup, you must keep in mind that everything you aim at requires specific actions with their associated costs. These can be costs of time, a required sacrifice of a favourite activity, a long-time habit, or a family tradition. In business, you have to accept not being understood or popular until you prove your point. The subject matters are countless. But remember that you will not only have to sacrifice but continually compromise, as nothing is self-standing. When the need for compromise is recognised instead of seen as a frustration, you will remember your LM prototype down-force and drag issue. None of that exists when you are on the pit lane; only at high speed does it manifest. Therefore, you are experiencing the symptoms associated with the movements of high performance, and you should be glad about that. It may not be pleasant, but unless you were in motion of some sort, it would not be happening.

Rules, regulations, and procedures are high down-force mechanisms. They cause actions to be specific and create grip in any organisation, including a family. The drag effect is that creativity and personal touch may not be easily expressed, which creates a pack of potentially frustrated individuals if "down force" is too strong. That kind of drag will impose itself on the overall result of your lap time. So once again, determine the factors of influence in your results, and organise them to create the best compromise possible for high-speed results.

High inspiration, a spirit of care, and individual consideration are high-speed and low-drag systems. They may give much-needed uplifting motivation, but if you are low on down force, you are therefore low on grip and will tend to spin your wheels through the corners. You will have a hard time keeping your best race lines in place, therefore losing overall high performance. The solution? Once again: track specific and relevant compromise. This is why there is no one-size-fits-all solution in any personal or organisation matter. Every organisation has a certain pulse and culture, an overall identity that will require a certain level of compromise. What we do in our family, although it works wonders for us, may not necessarily work in another family. There are applicable principles, but recipes are not always the same. Ultimately, great cooks don't read other people's cookbooks; they write their own. They first learn by applying what other cooks have done, and then they discover their very own, creating their own signature cooking. That has nothing to do with racing, but I think it makes the point. Besides, a good meal after the race is an awesome experience, a well-deserved ending!

Sometimes I hear: "I tried what you said, but it does not work for me." The point here is: stop trying and keep on doing. Keep changing and adapting until you find your own setup for high performance. You cannot simply and somewhat mechanically duplicate someone else's success. You will learn the principles, but you will discover for yourself what works for you. The wonderful news here is that you are totally unique and so is your success. Never give up; keep searching for the right setup adjustments.

No one has the complete answer to all of your problems or the complete system to create the life you always dreamed of in 90 days. Although many foundational truths are common to all successful people and successful organisations, at the end of the day, there are compromises in setup and aerodynamics that fit you and you alone.

WATCHING THE CLOCK

CHAPTER 52

We are now coming to the last chapter of the *Impossible Speed* book. I trust that by now, you have started to implement some acceleration strategy and that you are experiencing some increased measure of high performance in your life and/or your business. We are about to touch on a master subject here, so please slide into your high-performance prototype cockpit, strap in, and enjoy the ride.

There is an ultimate currency that is both the fuel and the judge of virtually all achievements. That currency is equally divided among all people on planet earth, rich and poor alike. That currency is not subject to inflation or deflation, and it equips and sanctions the great and the lowly on the same plane. Time is that currency.

Time is what separates winners and losers. In world-class racing, thousandths of a second can mean victory or defeat. The higher you climb on the ladder of achievement, the more significant becomes the time factor. And lest we forget, one day we will run out of time.

Looking back on our lives, we will not look with regret at how we did what we did as much as how we used our time during this life. Did we use it to build our ego, our own little empires, or did we use it to build our contribution so that others will get more out of their own time? Did we learn to be powerful, or did we learn to love and serve others? One day there will be only an answer, not a question anymore, not a second chance – time will be gone.

I am by no means trying to scare anyone; I simply want to cause us to think differently about the gift offered to us so that we honour it and make the most of it. Impossible speed is not about cramming everything you can into life before you die. It is about living to your utmost responsibilities and potential in the context of the time that is given to you. And if I can contribute more during my time, I want to learn to go faster towards that reality.

It is said that some people live like they will never die, while others die like they never lived. What a tragic statement. I am not sure who painted that picture, but unfortunately it is too often accurate. However, we have a choice – remember, it is never too late to change your setup and review your aerodynamic compromise! In the snap of a finger, you can decide to start changing how you will handle things from now on.

I recently heard the story of a 55-year-old man who decided to consider time differently. He calculated that if he lived for another 20 years, until the age of 75, his time left would amount to 1,040 weeks. He bought 1,040 marbles and placed the marbles in a jar. Every week on Saturday, he took one marble out and placed it in another jar. Religiously, he never missed counting his marbles. He was a radio talk-show host, and he relayed his story on the air. On that particular Saturday, the man had taken his last marble out of the jar. He knew that for each and every one of us, the day would come when we take our last marble out of the jar. The man said over the radio, "Today I took my last marble out of the jar. I lived long enough to take each marble out of the jar, 1,040 of them. I have had a long and blessed life, and as far as I am concerned, if I live another day, that will be a bonus that God will grant me."

Somewhere, a man was listening to the radio talk-show host and was deeply moved by this poignant story. He was a busy executive, successful in his own right. In his beautiful house were his wife and his son, and he was about to leave to the office for another day of work over the weekend. For a long time he had worked six days a week and was seldom at home the rest of the week to be with his family. Upon hearing the radio host, he realised that he was moving quickly towards the regret of not having made good use of his time. He ran upstairs and woke up his wife and said, "Honey, wake up and get ready; we are going out for breakfast." His wife was delighted and asked him the reason for it. He said that he had been so busy for so long and that he realised how little time he had given to her and their son, and he wanted to change that. And he said, "By the way, after breakfast, let's stop at the toy store. I want to buy a thousand marbles."

Life is not so much about what we don't have, but how we care for what we do have. Too often, it takes tragedies to make our roads safer, it takes divorce to realise the value of marriage, it takes illness and death to realise the value of relationships, it takes a broken heart to realise the value of love. Please make every effort to ensure that none of that applies to you, and if it does, use your impossible-speed knowledge to accelerate towards fullness in life. Choose to not squander time any longer. Why cry when you were born to rejoice?

If you apply the principles revealed in this book, you will acquire a fresh life perspective, you will utilise the fullness of your God-given potential, and you will grow and develop with meaningfulness and purpose. Your overall level of success and significance will take on a new dynamic and cause you to accelerate with impossible speed.

You were born with the capital of a champion. Right now, in the very depths of your heart, you have resources to cause you to find your life's true desire, your purpose, and your contribution. You have been given tremendous power to influence the course of your life to levels of performance that would make any glorious Le Mans prototype look pale in comparison. They may host the principles of high speed and high performance, but you drive them and embody them. People have imagined, designed, and built race cars as a form of the expression of life principles important to them. Live every day of your life doing the same thing: seek first and you will find, ask and you will be given – know that the door will open. No matter what your situation is like today, put the champion within you at the control of the race of your life and race like a winner.

■ RACING STRATEGIES TO CREATE HIGH PERFORMANCE

As a person, there is no one like you and there never will be. As a businessperson, you have enormous capabilities to solve any problem with which you are faced as you tap into your racer modalities and accelerate towards the results you want. Never fall victim to patterns of overindulgence and under-contribution. Build value in everything that you do, and there will be more than enough for you.

As men and women recognise the gift of life placed within them that is seeking expression in this world, they recognise that they belong to a higher reality – God's reality. Those who recognise and accept the glorious dimension of life will see their gifts and talents converge in a powerful demonstration of acceleration towards a future that they have not even dreamed of. That future belongs to the courageous and the humble, to the giver and not the taker. A life of realised values before capital gains, a life of contribution before enrichment, a life of power not resignation, a life of difference not conformity, a life of virtue before pleasure, a life that acknowledges that all that we have has been given to us, including our every breath.

Are you ready to purpose shift and become who you were born to be and accelerate all of your results in your personal life and in your business?

It is going to be the race of your life, and you will amaze yourself as you create your own high performance and achieve beyond your wildest dreams!

Let's race together to the **FINISH LINE!**

IT IS GREEN FLAG TIME!
GREEN, GREEN, GREEN!

BONUS:
INTERVIEW WITH TERRY BORCHELLER, DECEMBER 2009

Terry Borcheller is an accomplished sports-car race driver from Vero Beach, Florida. He is the newly minted overall winner of the prestigious ROLEX 24 at Daytona alongside the entire Action-Express racing team. This particular win means finishing ahead of America's greatest race teams and greatest drivers, such as Jimmie Johnson, Helio Castroneves, Juan-Pablo Montoya, Scott Pruett, Ryan Hunter Ray, etc. Terry is grateful for the privilege, humbled by the experience, and is already preparing for the next race with his attention focused on the 2010 Grand-Am Daytona Prototype championship.

Terry Borcheller, racing in LMGT1, stood on the podium of one of the world's greatest motorsports events: The 24 hour of Le Mans in France. He has won six professional championships, including 1998 SCCA Speed World Challenge, 2001 American Le Mans GTS Champion, and 2003 Grand-Am DP Champion; he has scored 60 professional wins in his career thus far. Demonstrating the attitude of a committed champion, Terry Borcheller put an end to a long winless streak with the 2010 Rolex Daytona 24 win. What an end to the drought!

Edrick: Terry, thank you for being with us today. Have you always had a clear, established vision in your mind of becoming a professional race driver?

Terry: I would not say that it was a clear and established vision, but it is something that I always wanted to do from the time I was very young.

Edrick: How young are you thinking back?

Terry: Probably five or six years old. I wanted to race motorcycles, but my mom was a little nervous about the idea. I ended up building my own race track in the woods around our house and started racing the other kids in the neighbourhood. At the age of twelve, I got my first go-kart for Christmas.

Edrick: Thinking of your level of competitiveness, when did you develop the mindset of a winner?

Terry: It is hard to put a time frame on it. It was always part of me; from the very first race I did, I had a passion to win. I don't even know how to explain it. I was leading my first race, but because of my inexperience, I ended up crashing big and flipping out of my kart. From as far back as I can remember, I have always been passionate about winning. I gained a lot of experience through Karting, winning a WKA National Championship in 1983. I had a great opportunity to become an instructor at the Bob Bondurant School of High-Performance Driving in 1990 that really helped me in every facet of the racing world. I felt that I already knew how to race, but the school gave me tons of seat time and a chance to learn the business of racing. Although I already knew how to win, I learned more about the whole world of motorsports and how to find the edge quickly, which I knew I would need to compete at the next level. There were a lot of elements that I needed to put into place, especially to learn how to differentiate myself from thousands of other guys who like me, wanted to become professional racers. I picked the brain of seasoned professionals like Johnny O'Connell. I took notes, asked questions, and really paid attention. I have learned a lot since those early days but still pass on some of those valuable lessons to others who consistently ask me how I did it.

Edrick: Other than winning, what allows a racer to attract sponsorship money?

Terry: Most racers are dependent upon their performance. If you can come up with a plan that allows everyone involved to experience a win-win, you've got a great sponsorship package. Rarely does a company want to throw money at a car, team, driver, whatever, for a sticker on the side of the race car. You must prove the value of the sponsorship dollar, and this can be very difficult to do. NASCAR has it figured out. Your performance as a driver is not always the dominating factor. If you just get in the show, sponsors win.

Edrick: Do you have a specific system that allows you to succeed as a racer?

Terry: When I coach people I always tell them, the more professional of a level you get into, the more intense it is. My approach is to always be ready and always be in the best possible condition. You cannot predict the outcome of races; you can do everything right and things can still go wrong, or you can do wrong things and end up having an amazing day (rarely)… For me as a driver, it is about functioning the best I can in all three dimensions: body, soul, and spirit. My body – exercise and nutrition are really important. I have made a lot of sacrifices over the years to try and be in the best shape possible. I want to always be at my best and never waste any opportunity and regret it because I did not prepare properly. For that reason, although I love certain things such as coffee, chocolate, a nice glass of wine, I abstain from them during race weekends and limit it during other times. Your soul, your mind, your emotions: for me it is first to follow God's principles that are found in the Bible. To make sure that my priorities are right with my wife and my children. Winning in the race car and losing my family would not allow me to consider myself a winner. Spiritually, my walk with God comes first, and every time I sit in that race car, I say, "Give me wisdom, and thank you for allowing me to be here." I know there are many more purposes for me being in the racing community other than just racing. I also know that the doors have been opened by God, and He can close them at any time, and I'm okay with that. Racing is not where my identity comes from as a human being, even though it is a big part of my life. Everything that I need and everything that I am are found in my relationship with Jesus Christ. This has taken me a long time to understand, and I still don't always get it right, but it sure helps me to keep things in perspective at home and at the race track.

Edrick: Impossible speed is about personal growth first, then the outcome takes care of itself. First you have to start with your purpose and passion; would you agree with that?

Terry: Absolutely, because within our passion – for me that is in knowing the will of God; that is where I find my balance. It's not all about the racing, although it is very important to me, and winning is a big thing, and I give it all I have, to the race and to the team, because this is my commitment as a professional, and there is also huge satisfaction.

Edrick: What is most appealing to you in racing?

Terry: That is about the chequered flag, being first, and about the strategy. For me it's not about personalities, not even first about speed or cars; it's about the strategy to outsmart and out-think the competition. It is like a chess match. Finding the best setup, getting me and the car to perform at our best. Even if the cars are similar, trying to find an edge; it's about the details. Most races are not necessarily won on the last lap; the win is sometimes the fruit of a lot of hard work. It is really exciting. The flip side is that sometimes things just don't work out, like I had to deal with for an extended period of time. When things were not working, I went through this period in which I could not even buy a win. But it was in a time like this that I was able to solidify my purpose, develop my trust in God, and keep on going.

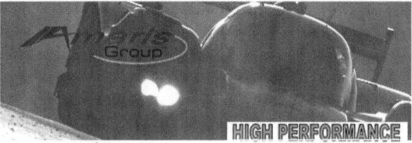

www.amarisgroup.ca

Hi there! This is Edrick Dunand!

It has been wonderful having you on the journey of High Performance through the pages of Succeed with Impossible Speed.

As you have discovered, good advice does not tell you what to do, but helps you discover your own "high performance modalities" so you can create your own "Impossible Speed".

I trust that now you want to go further, and implement the laws of "Impossible Speed" in order to create the results you want personally and professionally, or in your organisation.

As your High Performance partner, let me introduce you to:
- **The Amaris Group**, and its unique approach to leadership development
- **Amaris Racing**, bringing racing power to your marketing, your boardroom and your staff.

Helping you achieve High Performance is the complete focus of the Amaris Group. Our Leadership Development company capitalises on the power of World Class Racing principles and brings them to you and your company.

Our commitment is to see you or your organisation through to new levels of achievement and fulfillment, and develop pre-eminence in your field or industry.

Whether you want to run in house training or join us for life altering events on the race track we will help you develop your staff's "racing edge".

You may also be interested in entering the racing scene with us and becoming an official partner of Amaris Racing and its success story. Amaris Racing will bring your corporate message to the track. We will create a unique environment for a **high appeal and privileged leadership development platform for executive and employee training!**

www.amarisgroup.ca

NEXT STEP! Benefit from the message of "Succeed with Impossible Speed" in your personal, professional and organisational performance.

The **Amaris Group team** brings you a full range of High Performance Training based on the "Impossible Speed" systems.

Amaris Group - Leadership Development

High Performance Training
- Sales Performance Training
- Service Performance Training
- Executive Performance Training
- Motorsports Themed Multisensory Learning
- On track Development Events
- Dynamic and Content Rich Employee Rewards and Recognition

Human Dynamics Consultancy
- Executive Coaching
- People Change Management
- Employee Development Coaching
- Conflict Management
- Individual Profiling
- Organisational Profiling
- Merger and Acquisitions HR profiling

www.amarisgroup.ca   1 866 211 1189

Motorsports Investment Strategy

Our Motorsports Investment strategy is designed to empower your brand. By partnering with Amaris Racing, we enable you to associate your business with two of the most powerful decision influencers: **High Level Sporting Achievement and Story Based Inspiration.**

Amaris Racing is delighted to make available its various racing programs, from entry level to our future World Class Racing circuits. Our goal is to create a **superior ROI by a maximised use of our racing platforms.**

Motor Racing is a prestigious and extremely dynamic environment. It generates awe inspiring responses from racing fans and car enthusiasts alike, and reaches across a wide spectrum of the marketplace. Capitalising on the high impact of motor racing is a sought after strategy utilised by countless leading organisations who want to strategically position their image and influence their market.

Amaris Racing is adding to this already successful approach to Motor Racing a new business success catalyst: integrated human resources training and leadership development. We empower individuals and organisations by equipping them with the "High Performance Models" of World Class Racing.

This convergent approach between Marketing, HR Training, and strategic branding based on World Class Racing opens the way to a powerful business momentum building.

To request a complete information package, please contact Edrick Dunand directly at 1 866 211 1189 – ext. 721 or email edrick@amarisracing.com.

www.amarisracing.com

Need a dynamic and thought provoking speaker?

"Often times, people and organisations simply need a fresh perspective to empower them to get the results they want."

Edrick Dunand will bring you one of the many topics included in "Succeed with Impossible Speed" on personal and team performance.

With his unique blend of experience in business, motor racing and high performance philosophy, Edrick will cause your people to think afresh.

Known for his inspirational style, Edrick has an uncanny ability to stir people to look at defining result factors which can be overlooked or go undetected.

To book Edrick for your next event, please call
1 866 211 1189, Ext.721

www.amarisgroup.ca

Edrick drives his audience to understand the power of heart level thinking as a catalyst of high performance and breakthrough capability.

Change is the accelerating constant of our world, and staying ahead of the competition requires a new type of thinking: the way of "Impossible Speed"!

Edrick Dunand is a Member of Toastmasters International

For more benefit from the "Impossible Speed" educational series and events….

- Volume orders
- Product updates

Please visit:

 www.impossiblespeedliving.com

Amaris Group – 1866 211 1189

LaVergne, TN USA
11 August 2010
192993LV00002B/2/P